Paramotoring

from the ground up

Paramotoring
from the ground up

Noel Whittall

Airlife
England

First published in the UK in 2000
by Airlife Publishing Ltd

British Library Cataloguing-in-Publication Data
A catalogue record for this book is available from the British Library.

ISBN 1 84037 105 6

Editing, design and layout by Asgard Publishing Services, Leeds

Illustrations: Paul Thompson, Philip Gardner, Colin Fargher

Printed in Hong Kong

Airlife Publishing Ltd
101 Longden Road, Shrewsbury, SY3 9EB, England

E-mail: airlife@airlifebooks.com

Website: www.airlifebooks.com

Acknowledgements

I owe a debt to many people in the para-motor world who have contributed to this book – not always knowingly! Particular mention must be made of:

Scott Armitage
Reg Bradley
Mike Campbell-Jones, Reflex
Michel Carnet, Sky Systems
Mark Dale, BHPA
Chris Dawes, Airways
Gary Eato
Phil Gardner
Jolyon Harrison, Northern Paramotors
Richard Meredith-Hardy, BMAA
Leonard Newnham
Colin Nicholson, BHPA
David O'Donnell, BPC
Peter Price, XC/Windtech
Jon Radford, Rad Aviation
Lt Col (R) Basir Rahman
Simon Taylor
George Tyler
Matthew Whittall
Rob Whittall

I am grateful to the BHPA and the CAA for permission to reproduce extracts from their publications.

Photo credits

All photographs by the author except:
Jolyon Harrison 50, 51
Jon Radford 163
David Wootton 59, 82, 109

Contents

Introduction

The first time you see someone strap on a paramotor, start up and fly away from a field at little more than walking pace, the procedure can seem almost magic. Can you *really* do that? Is the age-old dream of flying as accessible as this? Yes!

Now project your imagination forwards a few weeks: you are sitting in a comfortable seat suspended under your own paraglider wing on a summer evening as the countryside passes slowly a few hundred feet below. The small motor behind you is running easily at about half power. Your destination field is a couple of kilo-metres away, and slightly to the right. Course correc-tion needs no more than a slight lean of your body, and a minute or two later you watch the fence slide by, maybe a hundred feet beneath your boots. Throughout your flight you have been taking note of anything which reveals the direction of the wind at ground level – smoke from barbecues, flags, washing on lines, movement of crops. Now you let the motor idle as you reduce height in a curve which brings you round to face exactly into the wind, turning just by pulling gently on one of the control lines. You are approaching the middle of the field now, looking down and checking that there is no sideways drift. No: you're flying dead straight and sinking fast enough to know that there will be plenty of room left for landing. OK, cut the power completely and glide to a perfect dead-engine touch-down, stalling the wing at the last moment so that no more then a single step is needed. After landing, the complete aircraft is packed up and ready to put in a car within ten minutes.

Opposite *A good all-round paramotoring outfit of the mid-90s: an Adventure Perf wing and F3 power unit*

9

You can do it. Flying a paramotor is achievable by anyone who has reasonable physical co-ordination and the patience to learn properly. The flight described above could be at the start of a flying career which might take you into trying to break long-distance records, into regular competition flying at home or abroad, or even adding an extra dimension to an interest such as archaeology. The cost is comparable with running a small motorcycle.

I have to add that this activity depends on the weather, so as well as those fine summer evenings or clear winter days there will also be some frustrating periods when the wind and rain keep you grounded.

This book will reveal many of the things which will help you to become a safe paramotor pilot. It should also help you to avoid the many pitfalls along the route. However, don't be lulled into the idea that it is a substitute for skilled instruction in the art. **I cannot stress strongly enough that good professional teaching is essential, and that reluctance to spend whatever it costs is false economy indeed.**

A tandem flight with a qualified instructor is a great introduction to paramotoring. Here the author is taken up by Chris Dawes at the Airways flying school.

How safe is it?

Is it safe? This is the most commonly asked question, and the honest answer is 'No'. The presence of gravity means that any form of aviation involves an element of danger which is absent in land-bound activities. But, of course, that is not the whole answer, and one of the things that distinguishes a *pilot* from someone who merely operates a flying machine is the constant ability to recognise risk and eliminate it. If you learn properly, understand the aircraft's limitations and respect the elements, the danger involved in paramotoring is very small indeed. Compared with the rewards, I believe the danger is completely within acceptable limits.

How it started

To know the history of the paramotor, we have to know how paragliders have developed. The whole idea of flying parachutes rather than simply falling out of aircraft with them dates back only to the 1960s, when first the Para Commander (PC) and then the rectangular ram-air canopies were introduced. The PC was an elaborated single-surface round canopy, but it moved forwards fast enough to develop some lift. Its performance was soon overtaken by the ram-airs, which are double-surfaced and consist of a number of airfoil-sectioned cells with openings at the front which allow them to inflate as they move through the air. They were much more efficient than any of the round canopies, and it wasn't long before people began to experiment with gliding down hills with them. The paraglider was born.

The first law of aviation development is that nobody is ever satisfied for long. Quite soon after the ram-airs arrived, people started to apply power to them. The earliest version I recall was the Para Plane, from the USA, which was rather like a propeller-driven go-kart attached to a big ram-air canopy. Contemporary testers reported that it climbed quite well but forward speed was painfully slow – not surprising, bearing in mind the early state of development of dynamically-inflated wing technology.

A very simple jump-type canopy, which was the starting point for modern paragliders.

Naturally, development continued, and such soft wings with wheeled structures have developed greatly. However, because they are not foot-launched, in the United Kingdom they fall within the Microlight Flying Regulations. These are very much more strict than the regulations for foot-launched aircraft, and are outside the scope of this book.

Back-pack power units had been tried during the early days of hang-gliding. The early experiments were not very successful – the rear rigging wires of a hang-glider were inevitably just where the propeller needed to be – and the back-packs were soon superseded by motors fixed to the structure of the glider rather than to its pilot. However, when it came to driving the floppy wing of a paraglider, the back-pack arrangement came into its own at last.

And all that is just what this book is about: learning to fly a soft wing, and then mastering the skills and subtleties involved when you add a simple power unit.

Some of the information on the gliding part of the sport owes much to my earlier book *Paragliding: the Complete Guide* (Airlife Publishing). If you can fly a paraglider already, there will be parts of the text that you can skip: I really have tried to introduce the sport 'from the ground up'.

Noel Whittall 1999

A great freedom

Permission to fly

We are allowed to fly paramotors within the United Kingdom with a minimum of red tape, thanks to the CAA Foot-launched Powered Aircraft (FLPA) Exemption, Schedules 1, 2 and 3. From here on we'll just call it 'the Exemption'. It covers both powered paragliders (PPGs) and powered hang-gliders (PHGs). It is a very useful and valuable piece of paper for us to have, because it allows us the freedom to fly aircraft that escape the vast number of rules, regulations and inspections with which even slightly heavier machines must comply. Note also how clumps of initials creep into the vocabulary as soon as flying is involved.

The Exemption did not just suddenly appear; it is the result of years of diligent work by the British Hang Gliding and Paragliding Association (BHPA) and the British Microlight Aircraft Association (BMAA). It is reviewed regularly, and provided we operate without drawing adverse publicity, its continued renewal should not be a problem. However, if just a few stupid or thoughtless pilots operate dangerously, our privilege could disappear very quickly.

On page 14 is an extract from the Exemption which covers the all-important matters of just what you can and cannot do. It is very straightforward, and is introduced here so that nobody taking up the sport will be in any doubt about what the restrictions are. Existing paraglider pilots will find that some of the rules are tighter than they have been used to when just gliding.

Schedule 3 to Foot-launched Powered Aircraft Exemption
Operating conditions for foot-launched powered aircraft

1   The pilot shall be aged 16 years or over.

2   The aircraft shall be foot-launched.

3   The aircraft shall not be flown:

   (i)   for public transport or aerial work other then aerial work which consists of the giving of instruction in foot-launched powered flying machines;

   (ii)   by night;

   (iii)   other than in sight of the surface and subject to the flight visibility and cloud clearance requirements given in Table 1 [see page 16];

   (iv)   over any congested area of a city, town or settlement;

   (v)   closer than 500 feet to any person, vessel or vehicle or structure except while it is landing in accordance with normal aviation practice or while hill soaring with the engine stopped;

   (vi)   during take-off within 500 feet of a structure (which the pilot could reasonably expect to be inhabited) unless the structure is either the property of the pilot or prior permission has been obtained from the occupants;

   (vii)   when towing any article (including any glider);

   (viii) within any Aerodrome Traffic Zone unless with the permission of the appropriate Air Traffic Control Unit;

   (ix)   within Controlled Airspace: or

   (x)   within any Prohibited, Danger or Restricted Area.

4   No person shall cause or permit an article or person to be dropped from the aircraft;

5   Notwithstanding Rule 17, such aircraft shall yield the right of way to all other aircraft. In the event of two such aircraft converging, the aircraft which has the other on its right shall give way; further, if approaching head-on or approximately so and there is a danger of collision, each shall alter its course to the right.

The CAA Exemption applies
strictly to foot-launched aircraft
like this lightweight Revolution
(below). It doesn't cover any
aircraft using a wheeled
undercarriage, such as this
Kestrel (left), or its American
cousin the Buckeye.

AIRSPACE	FLIGHT VISIBILITY	DISTANCE FROM CLOUD
Class A to Class E	Flight prohibited	Flight prohibited
Class F & Class G	Above FL 100 approx. 10,000 ft	
	8 km	1000 ft vertically and 1500 m horizontally
	At or below FL100 above 3000 ft AMSL	
	5 km	1000 ft vertically and 1500 m horizontally
	At or below 3000 ft AMSL	
	3 km	Clear of cloud

Table 1: Flight visibility and cloud clearance requirements

Respect air law

The fact that you do not have to hold a licence to fly a paramotor does not mean that you have the freedom of the skies. You are bound by air law in just the same way that a cyclist is bound by the Road Traffic Acts.

Qualification

The information in this book will help you to get the BHPA's Power PG rating. This is not a licence, simply a certification of competence, but it is fairly essential for getting reasonably priced third-party insurance. It is also the gateway to participation in certain levels of competition.

Although it is legal to operate a paramotor in the UK without a rating or insurance, it is obviously not a good idea. Further, in these increasingly litigious times, it is easy to imagine the detrimental effect of finding yourself in court for a minor dispute concerning your flying and having no way of showing that you are competent to use your paramotor.

Paramotoring Code of Practice

The BHPA's Code of Practice is straightforward and short. Naturally, much of it is concerned with ensuring that you don't operate your paramotor in a way which causes nuisance to others. It is mainly just social common sense aimed at preserving the Exemption. Here are the main points :

- Don't fall foul of the law of nuisance by repeatedly taking off near dwellings.

- If you use a particular field frequently, vary the flight path often. In particular, do not persist in trying to make headway against the wind when this will keep you within sight and sound from the ground for minutes on end.

- Generally, avoid existing hang-gliding and para-gliding sites. Most of them have been negotiated with the landowners on the understanding that the activity is silent.

- Always do all you can to avoid disturbing livestock. Avoid bird sanctuaries and riding stables.

- Contact the landowner if you land out.

- Respect the Country Code.

Display flying

Once word gets around that you have a paramotor, you are quite likely to be asked to demonstrate it at all sorts of functions ranging from school sports to air displays. Do not accept. It may be possible, but the laws on display flying are strict and you have to do a lot of groundwork first. Your proposed display must first be approved by a Display Authorisation Evaluator appointed by the CAA. The BHPA will put you in touch with an evaluator who can deal with FLPAs.

*A lone PPG shares the air with
a flight of microlights.*

Introducing the aircraft

The flying machine

A paraglider wing looks like a rather complicated dead tent until air blows into the openings at the front of its cells. This produces sufficient internal pressure to shape the fabric into an efficient flying structure capable of generating enough force to lift you off the ground. You have to learn to manage this on its own before adding power.

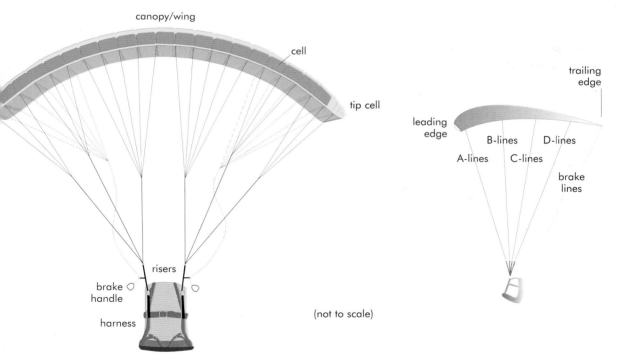

Figure 1: A simplified paraglider. The wing is built up of many cells joined together side by side. A trainer may have about 30 cells, while a high-performance competition wing may have up to 100. Except at the tips, each of the cells has a port in the leading edge through which it is inflated as the wing moves through the air. The cell walls have holes cut in them to act as communication vents, so that the pressure can remain equal throughout the wing. The trailing edge is closed along its entire length.

19

A typical intermediate paraglider. This is the Windtech Ambar, from Spain. Like most wings designed in the late 1990s it can also be flown with a motor, although it is not specially designed for power.

The wing

The paraglider wing (often referred to as the canopy – a throwback to its parachute origin) is made from very high-quality coated nylon cloth. It is held in shape by internal air pressure. The air is admitted through the ports at the front of the cells, and as long as these holes are clear and facing the airstream, the wing will keep its shape. The positive internal pressure is quite low, but it is enough to retain the basic cross-section very effectively.

The Ambar has diagonal ribs, as this shot shows. Note also the openings at the leading edge of the wing, and see how the brake line fans out to join the trailing edge at several points.

If you are used to seeing the rounded edge at the front of a normal aircraft wing, it appears that the gaps at the front of the cells would make the paraglider airfoil very inefficient, but this is not really a problem. Once all the cells are full the air inside is virtually static, and there is a slight 'back-up' which causes a buffer effect at the leading edge. The resulting flow is surprisingly smooth.

The cell walls are usually reinforced at the front with Mylar, a stiff plastic material. This helps to keep the ports at the leading edge open at all times.

The cell walls have large ports cut in them so that air inside the wing can move between them with ease. This is very important, because it makes the wing easy to inflate in the first place and also allows the pilot to move air around within the wing in the event of a temporary deflation in flight. More about this in the next chapter.

The positioning of the cell walls – often called 'ribs' as in normal aircraft – and the positioning of the attachments for the lines determine the shape the wing takes up in flight when it is supporting the load of the pilot. Naturally, all these points are very carefully calculated, using complex computer-design techniques. Sometimes designers will set certain ribs at an angle so that they will take the load as directly as possible from the upper to the lower surface and on down the lines. These are referred to as 'diagonal ribs'.

Lines and risers

The lines are a necessary evil. They contribute nothing to the performance of the aircraft except drag, so designers try to use as few as possible. The risers are short strips of nylon webbing which join groups of lines to the harness. They keep the lines clear of your head during flight and are your primary source of control while ground-handling. On early paragliders each line went straight from the riser to the wing, but modern designs use a succession of branches in the lines. This has more than halved the overall length of line used in a typical paraglider from 800 metres in the early days to less than 350 metres now, with a corresponding reduction in drag.

The positions of the points where the lines join the wing play a huge part in determining the safety, speed and over-all handling of a paraglider. Also, they make all the difference in whether a particular model is easy to launch or not. I mention this here not because you can do anything about it, but so that you will be sure to try some differ-ent gliders before you decide which one to buy.

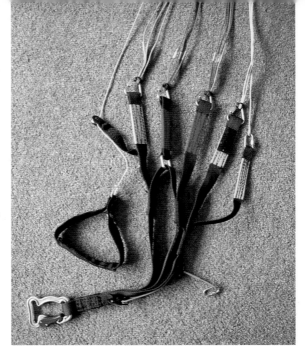

A set of risers and attachments from the Firebird Ignition, a typical intermediate paraglider which also behaves very well under power. Left to right: brake line (yellow), D-riser (green), C-riser (blue), B-riser (red), A-riser (yellow). Here the A-riser is split; the single yellow on the right attaches to the tip only, which makes it very easy to fold the tips in for rapid descent.The blue line is the connection for the speed system.

A paraglider depends on the weight of the pilot to match the other forces and keep the whole thing in flying configuration, so the position of the harness is absolutely critical too. The risers play an important part in determining this. On the simplest gliders there will be two pairs of risers. More advanced designs have three or even four pairs. By convention the front pair are referred to as the A-risers, the next as B-risers, and so on. You may see the expression 'split A-risers' in specifications for gliders. This means that the line run-ning out to the tip on each side has its own little sub-riser, which makes it easy for the pilot to fold the tips in during flight (see 'Big ears' on page 63).

Lines consist of a load-bearing core enclosed within a woven outer sheath. The most popular material is an aramid, such as Kevlar. It is now usual for sheaths of different colours to be used for the sets of lines, so that the 'A's can be readily distinguished from the 'B's and so on when laying the glider out. Some makes also colour-code the risers.

Right *Lines and risers are usually colour-coded. Here the blue tag shows the A-riser, but the colours vary from maker to maker.*

A selection of maillons and karabiners. Any such link that you trust your life to should have its maximum safe working load marked on it. Until quite recently this was usually in kilograms. However, they are now marked according to the international system (SI) in which the unit of force is the newton. There are 9.807 newtons to 1 kg-force. Ah, such progress.

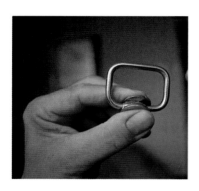

You can free off an obstinate maillon by using two coins to help grip the nut.

Maillons and karabiners

The lines are attached to the tops of the risers with link-rings closed by a screwed nut. These rings are often called *maillons*.

The bottoms of the risers are joined to the harness with karabiners or large maillons. My preference is to use karabiners because they are easier to detach at the end of the flying session. There are many different types, and it is essential to use those which have locking gates.

Brakes

Primary steering on paragliders is achieved by pulling down the trailing edge of the wing on the side to which you want to turn. The controls that do this are commonly called the *brakes*. They consist of a line on each side which fans out towards the top, to be sewn to the trailing edge at several points. The brake handles are attached to the rear risers with studs, magnets or Velcro when not in use.

Speed systems

All but the most basic paragliders now include a speed system. You will not use it until you are fully familiar with the handling of the wing.

At its simplest, a speed system is a mechanism which allows you to shorten the A-risers during flight. This reduces the angle at which the wing enters the air (the *angle of attack* – see page 30), which increases its speed. The usual way of doing this is by linking a pair of pulleys on each A-riser to cords which are routed down through the sides of the harness to a foot-bar or stirrup. A firm push on the stirrup draws the pulleys together and normally produces an increase in speed of about 6 kph. Lowering the front of the wing in this way does increase the chance of it tucking under if you meet turbulence, but the risk is extremely small unless you are using an advanced competition wing – something I would never recommend for paramotoring.

You may come across more complex systems for adjusting the angle of attack. Some models use compound pulleys which operate progressively on the A-, B- and C-risers so that the wing is virtually undistorted. Sometimes adjustment is also possible on the rear risers. These adjusters are usually called 'trimmers', and take the form of quick-release friction buckles which are operated manually: pulled down, they slow the wing. The big difference between trimmers and a foot-operated speed system is that the speed system can be released instantly if you hit turbulence – indeed, it is almost an instinctive reaction to release it – whereas trimmers inevitably take time to alter.

Some authorities recommend not using any sort of speed system when motoring, but I believe it is safe enough if you are flying a conservatively rated wing and are prepared to let it off in rough air.

So far, all my comments have applied to wings which have been designed originally just for paragliding. Mike Campbell-Jones' Reflex is different, because it was conceived from the beginning for use with power. The Reflex gets its name from the shape of its airfoil, the trailing edge of which curves upwards slightly to provide an elevator effect. This allows the wing to become more stable at speed, so even in rough air it can safely be flown with the trimmers right off and the speed system full on.

Harness
The design of the harness affects your comfort in flight as well as the way the wing responds to control inputs. The harness used when simply flying your wing as a glider will probably not be the same as the one you use with the motor. The main feature to take note of is the points at which the risers attach to it. On a gliding harness these will probably be fairly low on your chest, whereas the power harness may have them much closer to the shoulders. The higher they are, the harder it will be to turn the glider by shifting your weight.

The subtleties of harness design are complex and often a matter of personal taste. When you are starting, it is sufficient to appreciate that changing harnesses affects the flight characteristics of your glider, so be guided by experts until you have accumulated lots of experience.

Harnesses are normally equipped with a selection of pockets. These are very useful, but when motoring you have to be extra careful about dropping anything that you may pull out of them in flight. Naturally, items such as cameras and radios should be attached with cords or bungee rubbers, but not everything can be tied on. Virtually any known variety of chocolate bar, with or without peanuts, is capable of passing through the guard and damaging the propeller.

Testing and certification

Any paraglider you are contemplating entrusting your life to must have been submitted to a recognised air-worthiness procedure. This will have tested its load-carrying capacity by subjecting it to a shock test, and its flight stability in a wide range of conditions. There are two basic approaches to the matter of flight stability: the test pilots can assess the wing's resistance to collapse in flight, or test how readily it resumes shape if it does collapse. Don't get too anxious about the use of the word 'collapse'. Any small deflation of a part of a cell is called a collapse, and small ones are routine in rough air – they often pass unnoticed by the pilot.

The two main testing standards at the time of writing are the German-based DHV Gütesiegel procedure and the French-based AFNOR system. The German approach emphasises resistance, while the French is a bit more concerned with recovery. Both systems are well proven, but there is now a move to an overall European standard which combines their best features. Every wing that has been approved, by what-ever authority, will carry a stamp or label carrying the details. Have nothing whatever to do with any wing that is not stamped.

Trying it for size

A trial 'hang' is an essential part of buying a new flying harness of any type, and doubly so if a paramotor is involved. Don't just limit this to a couple of minutes on the dealer's rig: install a pair of hang-points at home if you can. All harnesses have a variety of adjustments, and it is infinitely better to get these set comfortably when dangling from the rafters of your garage than to discover, moments after becoming airborne, that they are in agony mode. But there is a lot more to be learned than just comfort settings. You will be able to tell whether the thrust-line of the motor will be horizontal during flight (as it should be) and to practise finding the foot-stirrup. You can get even greater value out of the exercise if you have an experienced pilot to help you. Failing that, a strategically placed mirror is the next best thing.

Don't be shy about doing these trial hangs with all your flying gear on – especially your helmet. This is particularly important if you favour the full-face variety, because you will discover that there are many things you can't see to check, such as the fastening of the chest strap, because the mouth-protecting part obscures your view. If you know about it, you can compensate.

If you have a reserve parachute, checking that you can find the deployment handle accurately every time is another thing to rehearse during trials. Also, try twisting round to look at the motor. You will be surprised at just how little you can see, and will appreciate how making significant adjustments while airborne would be virtually impossible.

If you decide to start the motor during a trial hang (and it's not a bad idea), check first that there are no loose articles which could be drawn into the prop, and beware of people who may be attracted to come and have a close look at the source of the commotion.

All these comments about airworthiness refer to the paraglider when it is flown without a motor. As soon as you add power, none of the airworthiness certification applies. This is because the loads the motor imposes, with its torque and shifting thrust-line, can easily take the aircraft outside any flight envelope the designer could plan for. My advice, therefore, is simple: choose a wing which is renowned for stability and learn to fly it as efficiently as you can. Don't be unduly alarmed by the fact that the airworthiness certification does not apply: modern wings are very stable and PPG accidents are much more likely to be due to pilot error than to aircraft failure.

Looking after the equipment

The materials of the wing and harness are durable, but care must be taken all the time. Ultra-violet radiation will degrade the canopy, so unnecessary exposure to the sun must be avoided. This is not such a big problem in Britain, but it certainly is in hotter countries. The efficiency of the wing depends on the coating which is rolled into the surface to make it impermeable to air. This is easily damaged by chemicals of many types. If the wing gets dirty, the best advice is to simply brush the dirt off as best you can. If you must, use a little clean water, but avoid all soaps, detergents and any other chemical cleaners.

Try not to keep the wing packed up really tightly for any length of time. If you have the space, keep it nicely relaxed out of its bag when storing it for more than a few days, so it can breathe enough to discourage fungal growth and also to avoid permanent creasing.

How does it fly?

Before we get involved with the power elements of paramotors, we have to understand how the wing part of the equation works. In other words, before you can para*motor*, you have to learn to para*glide*. Paragliders are such stable aircraft that it would be quite possible to fly one for years without having more than the vaguest idea of what keeps it in the air, but if you are going to use them safely you must understand some very basic aerodynamics. This is really very simple and straightforward stuff which many readers will be familiar with already, but if you are not it should enhance your appreciation of flight generally. It will also make it more likely that you will automatically react sensibly if you find yourself in a sticky situation. And, maybe not least, you will need this information to pass the BHPA exams required to obtain your pilot rating.

At first sight a floppy textile wing connected to the pilot's seat by a network of lines doesn't seem to have much in common with conventional aircraft, but in fact the forces which allow it to fly are exactly the same. We shall not delve very deeply into the world of aerodynamics or physics, but it does help to think about the nature of the air and what happens when objects are moved through it. Think of air as a relatively dense gas which has considerable mass and reacts in predictable ways when it is disturbed.

... floppy textile wings become transformed into flying machines.

Lift and drag

Lift

The upward force that makes the wing fly is *lift*, and can be measured in pounds or kilograms. The key to developing lift lies in the airfoil shape of the cell walls and the angle at which the airfoil meets the air. The walls are shaped as shown in Figure 2.

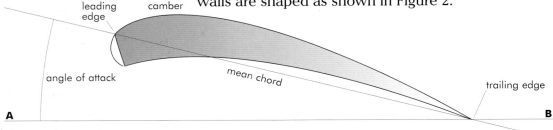

Figure 2: Airfoil section

Assuming that air is flowing past it from **A** to **B**, the airfoil generates lift in two ways:

1 By meeting the air at a positive angle of attack; that is, with the leading edge higher than the trailing edge. Any moving flat surface will develop lift if it is tilted in this way, because the pressure under it is raised by the force of the air pushing against it. This effect is easy to visualise, or to experience simply by sticking a hand out of a car window and varying its angle of attack. This form of lift is often referred to as plate lift; at the speeds we fly at, about one-third of the wing's lift is generated in this way.

Figure 3: Airflow past an airfoil. As long as the air keeps flowing past the airfoil smoothly, the pressure underneath will remain higher than that above, and the wing will respond by trying to move upwards into the lower-pressure region.

2 By being formed into a curved airfoil section. The shape causes the air passing over the top surface of the wing to take a longer path than air passing under the wing. This reduces the pressure on the upper surface. This type of lift can be called section lift. It is a powerful effect which normally contributes around two-thirds of the overall lift.

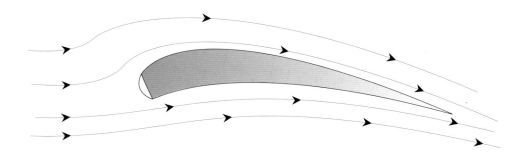

Gliding flight

How does a gliding wing keep moving through the air? It is obviously not being drawn through it by a propeller, so what does keep it moving along, and why does it stay up? The answer, paradoxically, is gravity: it doesn't really keep the paraglider up – it simply keeps it moving through the air in exactly the same way as it moves a skier downhill. While the glider is moving, the lift keeps the rate of descent low, but it is always there: gliders are always travelling 'downhill' through the air. The only way a glider can climb is to remain in air which is rising faster than the glider is sinking. The skill of the soaring pilot lies in locating such air and making the best of it.

If it appears odd to be dwelling on the skills of gliding in a book which is supposed to be all about paramotoring, please do not become impatient. When you add power to a paraglider, you will still be in a completely intimate relationship with the air, and appreciation of what it is doing around you is essential. Also, when the motor stops in flight, you instantly become a glider pilot whether you like it or not. I say *when* the motor stops, because sooner or later in your paramotoring career, you can be fairly sure that it will!

Drag

As well as producing lift as it moves through the air, a paraglider also produces *drag*. This also comes in two forms:

1 *Parasitic drag* is caused by the passage through the air of all the non-lifting parts of the glider. These include all the rigging lines, the risers, and, of course, the pilot. The main feature of parasitic drag is that, although small at low speeds, it very soon builds up as speed is increased. If you double the speed, you quadruple the amount of parasitic drag.[1]

2 Induced drag is induced by the passage of the wing itself through the air, and is a by-product of the way the airfoil develops lift. We saw that the combination of the angle of attack and the airfoil section produces a higher pressure below the wing than above

---

[1] The overall term 'parasitic drag' is a catch-all expression which includes several components, the greatest of which is profile drag. Keen pilots keep parasitic drag to the minimum by sitting back in the harness in flight and by wearing closely fitting clothing.

it, which generates lift. However, because of the pressure difference, the air close to the edges of the underneath of the wing naturally tries to migrate into the lower pressure above it via the tips and trailing edge. See Figure 4 to get a clearer idea of how this happens. This movement causes turbulence around the tips and trailing edge, and the turbulence causes drag. Unlike parasitic drag, this induced drag reduces as you go faster. The reasons for this are many and subtle, but it's easy to imagine in simple terms: *the faster the wing goes, the less time there is for any of the air it passes through to change direction and find its way into the low-pressure region above the wing.*

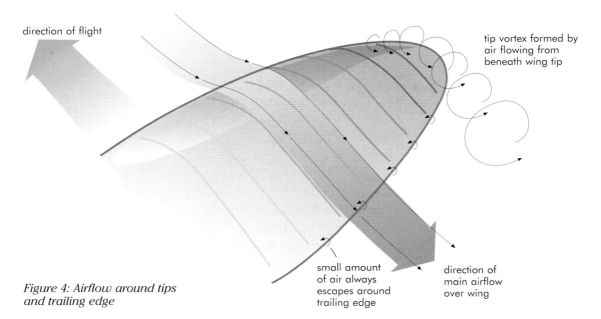

direction of flight

tip vortex formed by air flowing from beneath wing tip

small amount of air always escapes around trailing edge

direction of main airflow over wing

Figure 4: Airflow around tips and trailing edge

To work out the total drag of the aircraft at any particular speed, the figures for the two types of drag are added together.

Lift, drag and the glide ratio

Figure 5 shows how the development of lift and drag relates to the speed at which the wing is flying. Note that total drag is lowest at the speed at which the two drag curves cross. This is the speed which will give the most efficient gliding performance for that particular

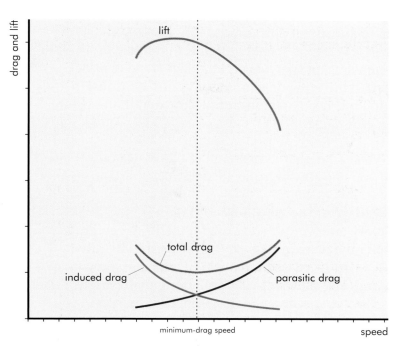

Figure 5: Graph of lift and drag against speed. The diagram shows, in simplified form, how the two types of drag alter with speed. When the combined drag is related to the overall lift developed by the wing, an impression of glide performance can be obtained.

wing. In the particular example shown in Figure 5, the lift is six times the drag at this speed. The point of interest in all this is that the ratio of lift to drag (l/d) also tells us what the gliding performance of the wing will be. The l/d ratio is effectively the same as the glide ratio, so in completely still air a paraglider with a best l/d of 6:1 will be capable of travelling forward 600 ft while descending only 100 ft. Needless to say, still air is rare indeed, as are the chances of flying at the optimum speed for the entire flight, but nevertheless l/d figures are useful as a general guide to performance.

Published l/d figures should always be treated with caution. They depend on the glider being flown at the optimum weight and were probably achieved with the pilot using a very low-drag harness. In any case, as soon as you add the extra drag caused by the paramotor power unit, the l/d will be degraded by anything up to 25 percent.

Minimum sink

Just as there is a speed (the *maximum-glide speed* or *best-glide speed*) at which any aircraft gives its best glide ratio, there is another one at which the sink rate is at its lowest. This is rather unoriginally called the *minimum-sink speed*, which is frequently reduced to 'min-sink'. It is achieved at a high angle of attack, when the wing develops maximum lift. Consequently minimum sink occurs at the slow end of the overall speed range.

When soaring, the best rate of climb will be achieved if you can stay in rising air while flying at min-sink.

Changing the angle of attack
Every time you operate one of the brake controls, you alter the angle of attack. Pulling them both down together increases the angle of attack of the whole wing. This slows the glider; if done with care, you can slow it to minimum-sink speed. Overdo it, and you may stall.

Apart from the brakes, the angle of attack may also be changed by operating a speed-system stirrup, which has the effect of lowering the leading edge by pulling the A-risers down. On other models the rear risers ('C's or 'D's) may be fitted with quick-release buckle devices which reduce the angle by allowing the rear of the wing to rise. These are called *trimmers*.

Stalling
To develop lift, a wing must disturb the air through which it passes, but the disturbance must be orderly. Air tolerates being forced to flow past an airfoil, chang-ing its speed and direction slightly to accommodate it, but continuing to flow in fairly straight lines. If it is forced to deflect too far, it will react by refusing to follow the surfaces smoothly, changing instead to a broken, turbulent flow. When this happens, lift imme-diately reduces dramatically and the wing is said to be stalled.

The most common cause of a stall is flying too slowly, but a wing can become stalled at any speed if the angle of attack is increased sharply enough.

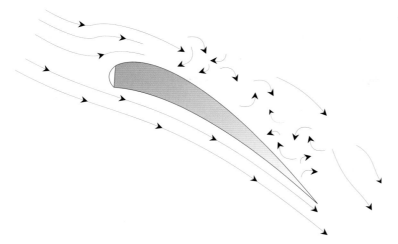

On any aircraft, stalling means loss of control and loss of height, so it is to be avoided. On a paraglider, the stall also means loss of pressure within the wing, with accompanying collapse. Naturally, this can be extremely dramatic, but fortunately it is easily avoided if you understand the possibility and fly accordingly.

Stalling paragliders is now recognised as being so dangerous that in many countries 'stall and recovery' is no longer a part of the required training syllabus.

The polar curve
The polar curve is a chart of the overall performance of your paraglider, plotting forward speed against rate of descent throughout its speed range. The axes of the graph are always drawn as shown in Figure 7. The minimum-stall speed and effective top speed show clearly, and you can tell at a glance the rate of sink at any speed in the range. By drawing a line from the zero point (where the axes cross) to form a tangent to the curve, you find the maximum-glide speed. Further, you can work out the most efficient speed to fly in different headwind conditions by drawing a similar tangential line from the point on the speed axis corresponding to the wind speed. A basic understanding of the way a polar curve reflects the behaviour of a glider at different speeds is very useful, but it is much more important that you learn to fly sensitively and sensibly, rather than merely by relying on instruments.

Of course, as soon as you apply power, the character-istics change. However, if you can visualise the polar, you will be able to fly efficiently. For example, using just enough power to maintain height while flying at maximum-glide speed should be the best way of covering distance in most conditions. You can see from this typical polar curve (Figure 7) that a para-glider's efficiency drops rapidly if you fly it fast. That means relatively high fuel consumption if you try to 'push' one when using a motor.

Note that a polar diagram describes the behaviour of the paraglider when supporting the ideal weight of pilot. A lighter pilot has the effect of moving the whole curve up and left a little, while a heavier one moves it down and right.

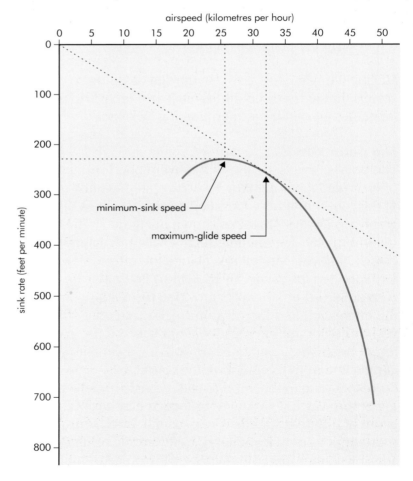

Figure 7: A typical polar curve

The controls

Paragliders are different. The basic controls are simple, but they have no exact counterpart on fixed-wing aircraft; I suppose 'independent flaps' would be about as close as you could get to describing them. They inherited the name 'brakes' from parachuting, and – although rather inaccurate – the expression is widely understood, so I have no conscience about using it throughout this book. One of the main skills to learn is to use the brakes smoothly at all times. Think of them as operating flexible guides for the air, not as machine-like levers or switches to be jerked on and off.

Your paraglider will be constructed so that if you sit comfortably in the harness and leave the controls alone it will fly in a straight line at around its best-glide speed. This is called 'trim speed'. On beginner and intermediate models this will also be its effective top speed.

Speed is adjusted by using both brakes simultaneously: typically, completely off for best-glide speed; one-quarter to one-third on for minimum-sink speed, and fully down to deliberately stall at the last moment for a light-wind landing.

When you look at a paraglider in flight, you will see how pulling the brakes causes the trailing edge to curve down. This increases the camber in the airfoil section and also increases the effective angle of attack. Increasing the camber and angle in this way increases the lift, which explains why pulling the brakes a little helps you off the ground after a launch run. It also allows you to slow the glider down to its minimum-sink speed when trying to stay in rising air. There are limits: increasing the camber too much results in a stall.

Basic steering is accomplished by pulling the brake down on the side to which you want to turn. This causes an immediate increase in drag on that half of the wing, and the glider begins to turn. This is simple to do, and looks logical when you watch it happening, but the dynamics of the manoeuvre are quite complicated. The section on roll and yaw (page 39) goes into this a little further.

Assuming that you start with both brakes on to some extent, tighter turns can be made by pulling further on one while releasing the other. This should not be over-done: insensitive heaving on the brakes could lead to stalling the inside wing and starting a spin, or winding up into an ever-tightening spiral dive.

On most models you can assist steering by leaning in the direction of the turn. This is called *weightshifting*.

Right *and* **opposite** *A Reflex being put into a tight left turn. See how the pilot is using weightshift to assist the turn.*

CHAPTER 3

Roll and yaw

Roll occurs when the wing is tilted sideways from the horizontal. *Yaw* occurs when the leading edge of the wing is not square on to the airstream.

When you change direction on a paraglider, both yaw and roll will occur, but it won't be very obvious unless you turn very tightly. This is because of the tremendous stability provided by sitting several metres below the wing.

One important effect of roll is that while the glider is turning, the minimum stall speed increases. The reason for this is the development of a centripetal force acting on the wing which effectively increases its loading (you feel it as a centrifugal effect which pushes you harder into the seat of the harness). Regardless of

the physical reasons, just remember that turning when flying very slowly is a very dodgy idea indeed which leads to stalls and spins.

Adjusting speed

I have explained that a paraglider will normally fly 'hands off' at its most efficient glide speed, or thereabouts. Much of the time you will want to go slower than this to make the most of rising air, so you pull down the brakes to some extent on both sides. This slows you down by effectively increasing the angle of attack. You could achieve a similar result by pulling the rear risers, although this is not recommended because it would be easy to pull too far and stall the wing. (It's useful to remember that you can use the rear risers this way in the unlikely event of a control line breaking.)

Increasing speed is another matter; you can make a slight improvement by putting your legs straight out in front of you and trying to keep drag to the minimum, but the only way to get a significant increase is by using a speed system (see page 24).

Design considerations

When considering how things fly, it is useful to keep in mind that you don't get something for nothing. When you improve one area of performance, there is usually a price to pay in another area. For example, a small wing may fly fast and handle well but have rather a high sink rate. It will also need to be flying fast to develop enough lift for take-off, which will make for tricky launches. If the wing is increased in size, the sink rate and launch performance may improve, but the top speed and easy-handling characteristics will quite likely be reduced.

All speeds are relative. Even compared with hanggliders, their nearest soaring relatives, paragliders are very slow aircraft indeed, and have a small speed range. This is not surprising really, when you consider how 'draggy' they are and that the drag increases according to the square of the speed.

Mastering the wing

One of the facts of paramotoring life is that you have to learn to fly a paraglider before going on to operate it in conjunction with motor power. This is not difficult, but the process is strange enough to warrant this complete chapter to itself.

It is apparently simple: just hang underneath the wing, which keeps inflated merely by gliding through the air. Easy. Until, that is, you find yourself standing by a confused mass of fabric and lines which somehow you have to get into shape above your head before going anywhere! Note that there must always be air moving past the wing if it is to gain and retain its shape. If there is a slight breeze it really is easy – you can stand still and let the wind do the work. In a calm, you have to work to drag the wing into the air.

Learning to paraglide needs a bit of patience. Somehow there rarely seems to be just the right amount of wind.

41

Once flying, you control direction by pulling the appropriate brake line, shifting your weight in the desired direction, or a combination of both. Control of speed is by using both brakes simultaneously, and landing requires little more than sensible judgement. However, the flying is the easy part: with paragliding, handling the wing on the ground and launching it is the tricky bit.

There are two methods of launching: forward and reverse. The forward launch is used when there is little or no wind. The reverse launch requires a light breeze, but has the great advantage of letting the pilot observe the wing throughout. Both styles require practice, but because weather conditions in the UK are rarely completely calm, we tend to concentrate more on the reverse technique.

Ground-handling

Reverse launch practice

You cannot spend too much time on the ground practising handling your wing. An hour or so getting really familiar with it on the flat will teach you more than any book can.

If there is a breeze of more than about 3 mph (5 kph) you should be able to try the preparation for reverse launching. To start with, restrict yourself to winds of no more than 10 mph (16 kph) – preferably less. Pick somewhere free from upwind obstructions such as trees or buildings so that the air will be smooth. Also, start in the upwind end of your field so that you have plenty of space if you get into difficulties.

Develop good methodical habits right at the start. For example, brake handles should be either in your hands or fixed to the risers (there will be studs or Velcro for this) and never just flopping about ready to tangle.

Wear helmet and gloves for all ground-handling and flying. The gloves are not an affectation: most paraglider pilots have collected friction burns from the lines at some time or other, and these are painful and long-lasting.

As with the rest of the book, this chapter is not intended as a substitute for professional instruction.

My descriptions here assume that you have a paraglider with the normal three-riser layout. However, the technique is basically the same with two risers (very unusual: only found on primitive training wings) or four risers (now normal on recent models). Just remember that in this book the 'A's are always the front risers and the 'C's or 'D's are the back ones.

Bearing in mind that you intend to become a paramotor pilot, the emphasis throughout your glider training must be towards complete control at all times, and particularly during take-off and landing. The sort of mistakes which may result in momentary loss of dignity with a paraglider will become much more important if you make them with twenty or thirty kilograms of working machinery strapped to you.

Learning good control is essential before trying to fly with a motor. Your first high hill launches will never be forgotten.

Pre-flight checks

Pre-flight checking must be a basic part of your flying from the very beginning. It is not something to do when you feel like it – do it every time. Good pre-flighting saves lives, usually your own.

At this stage you should not be taking the motor unit with you. See page 98 for pre-flight routines when using the motor.

Paragliding equipment inspection

Do this at the start of each day and routinely throughout the day.

Canopy: Correct size for pilot. All stitching sound. No broken or frayed lines. No obvious kinks.

Harness: Good condition with no fraying of webbing or stitching. Buckles correctly fitted and secure.

Riser attachments (maillons or karabiners): If steel – no rust. If alloy – no deep scratches. Fitted to harness so that the screws are inboard.

Brake lines: Handles firmly attached (use bowlines and tape the loose ends for extra security) and no obvious wear, particularly where the lines pass through guides or pulleys on the risers.

Helmet: Correct size and in good condition.

Pre-launch checks – *every time*

- Wind and weather: is it safe to fly?

- Helmet on and fastened

- Harness on and all straps secure

- Check leg-loops *again*!

- Lines and risers free and untangled

- Maillons/karabiners screwed shut

- Speed system (if fitted) connected

- Brake lines free and in the correct hands

- All clear above and behind?

- Wing: all cells inflated and under control

- All clear in front?

- Launch!

In-flight checks

Develop the habit of having a good look round the harness and canopy from time to time once airborne. A line broken by snagging on a rock during inflation is easily missed on the ground but will be obvious in flight.

Canopy inspections

At least annually – and preferably far more often – your canopy must be given a thorough inspection. This should be a cell-by-cell going-over, looking for worn areas and strained or broken stitching. It is also a good time to delve into it and remove any grass seeds, bits of twig or insects that may have found their way aboard. Run all the lines through your fingers, feeling for kinks or breaks, and check all their terminations.

Insect corpses are really bad news – they alone are good reason for very frequent clear-outs because they can release nylon-hostile acids as they decompose.

If there are bleached areas or other evidence of discoloration, have the canopy checked for UV degradation and porosity by a reputable dealer.

Laying the glider out

We'll assume that there is a light wind on the field today. Get the wing out of the bag and unroll it until you can check which is the leading edge and which is the trailing edge. Lay it so that it is on its back with the trailing edge directly into the wind. Now extend each side of the wing until it is all exposed. With any luck the lines and risers will be lying on the surface quite neatly and untangled near the trailing edge. If the harness is already attached, extend and lift the front risers a little to check that they are not twisted. At first it will be hard to tell, but as you gain experience it will soon become second nature. If the harness is separate, lead out each set of risers, check them for twists and tangles and attach them carefully. It is less confusing to set the harness in more or less the flying position and take the risers to it, than to move the harness to the risers.

Learning to form the wing into a stable wall before trying to pull it up

Whatever you do, be cautious. Even in a light wind the wing can easily get out of hand if you pull the front risers up too much.

CHAPTER 4

On most gliders the lines are colour-coded so that it is easy to distinguish the A-lines from the B-lines and so on. This is very helpful, but beware: there is no industry standard, so if you change gliders it is quite possible that yellow may be 'A' on one and 'C' on the other.

Now that everything is laid out, it is almost time to strap into the harness. But not before putting your helmet on! You should never be strapped into a glider without it. Doubtless it seems fussy, especially as the wind is light and you are definitely not going to attempt to take off. Never mind that: sooner or later you are certain to get dragged while practising ground-handling, and when that happens there is an excellent chance of meeting something head-first, so establish a 100-percent helmet habit right from the start.

Building the wall
OK, strap in and try 'building the wall'. You are going to be using the 'crossed-lines' method.

1 Start facing away from the wing.

2 Stay close enough to the trailing edge for all the lines to remain slack.

3 Make sure the risers on each side pass over your arms.

4 Detach and take hold of a brake handle in each hand.

5 Keeping hold of the brakes, grasp an A-riser in each hand too. Reach round the 'B's and 'C's to do this, so that they still pass over your arms.

6 Gently move forwards until you feel the lines begin to tighten a little. Look behind you to check that the lines are clear and untwisted, and then move so that they are slack once more.

7 You are now in the position you will need to make a forward launch, but we're not going to try that yet.

8 Make a half-turn (180 degrees), lifting one complete set of risers and lines over your helmet as you do so. Do not release the brake handles as you turn. Also, remember which way you turn, if you can – you will need to turn back the other way later.

9 You are now facing the glider. Move backwards, gently tightening the A-lines as you do so.

As the openings at the front of the cells meet the wind, be ready for the wing to try to inflate. It will build progressively to form a vertical 'wall', sitting on the trailing edge. If it feels as if it might get out of hand, you can keep control by moving towards the wing or by letting go of the 'A's and pulling both of the brake lines. However, in the light winds which you should be restricting yourself to as a novice, there should be no difficulty in raising and lowering the wall by leaning backwards and forwards so that your body does all the work.

Build a stable wall and experiment with the effect the brakes have on it. You will notice that when you pull the brake in your right hand, the left wingtip moves, and vice versa. This is very disconcerting at first and takes a bit of getting used to. Always keep hold of the brake handles and resist the temptation to change them over so that they feel 'right'. If you practise enough, this reverse brake effect will soon feel normal. The beauty of it is that when you turn around to launch, the brakes will automatically be in the correct hands. For ordinary paragliding this is a big advantage, and when you start to use the motor you will find that it is vital.

Very soon you will appreciate how you start the inflation of the wall by 'teasing' the cells open with gentle tugs on the A-lines, but once it is established you can control it by moving your upper body backwards and forwards. Getting used to the idea of using your whole body rather than just your hands and arms is an important lesson which will be very useful for the next stage …

Getting the wing flying

Once you are confident at controlling the wall you can move on to flying the wing. What you read here will, I hope, be helpful, as will the guidance of your instructor, but there is absolutely no substitute for the feel of actually doing it. Here we go, step by step again:

1 Build a good stable wall as described above, about a metre high, holding the A-risers just about where they join the lines.

2 Check that you are exactly upwind of the centre of the wing. See the panel on page 53 for clues and techniques to help you check this.

3 Make sure you are on a firm footing, with one leg forward of the other. Bend at the knees and hips.

4 Keeping hold of the A-risers close to the lines, coax them upwards rather than heaving. You pull with your shoulders more than your arms, which are really only guiding. The wing will climb, and as it does, you can let yourself be drawn under it. Your arms should be almost straight throughout the operation.

The wing will fly up quite easily. Too easily, probably, so that it overshoots and flops down all over you. Have another go, and then a few more. After a while you will learn at what point in the rise you need to stop pulling so that the wing stabilises at exactly the right spot above you. You will probably have to check it with the brakes to stop the overshooting.

When you have the knack of getting the wing inflated overhead, practise steering it gently while walking backwards. When it tries to go off to one side you should be able to keep it up by moving quickly under the centre of the wing.

In light winds you will be able to raise the wing without moving your feet significantly. However, you will soon find that when the wind is stronger you must move towards the wing as it comes up. It is hard to get the feel of just how much to move and how much to resist, but if you start the process by pushing your bottom against the seat and pulling through the harness, rather than just hauling with hands and arms, you will be well on the way to success.

Once the wing is up, concentrate on keeping it flying like a giant kite. At first it won't feel as if there is time to do anything, but soon you will discover how easy it is to keep it overhead by moving sideways so that you are always under its centre, and by checking it from overshooting with the brakes.

Below *and* **opposite** *Reverse pull-up – the author with a Firebird Ignition*

Getting the pull-up right during the reverse launch

As you draw the wing overhead, you must expect to have to move. If the wind is very light, you will have to move backwards to keep enough pressure in it. In stronger winds you will have to move towards it as it rises up.

This is a co-operative affair: if you heave too strongly and resist too much, the wing will overshoot and tuck. If you are too timid, it will 'hang up' halfway through its arc and drag you with it. If you run towards it too readily, it will collapse around you. When you get it just right, the action is smooth and easy and there seems to be all the time in the world to get centred under the wing and check everything before turning. Unfortunately books can only tell you about this: you have to learn it by practising.

The turn and the launch

With the wing flying happily above you, try to remember which way you turned at the start of the exercise (step 8 on page 48) and prepare to turn back the other way. Rehearse this. If you have forgotten or are completely confused (not at all unusual), there is a simple way of checking: look at the uppermost of the two sets of risers where they cross in front of you – the shoulder it comes from will be the one that must move backwards as you turn.

1 Take your time. Get the wing nicely stabilised above you, applying just enough brake to stop it going forwards. Then make the half-turn into the wind, lean well forwards and run.

2 As you go forwards you should raise your hands so that there is no pressure on the brakes. Power forwards, with your whole body pulling the wing through the harness.

3 Resist any temptation to 'help' your forward motion by trying to push the front risers. That would probably collapse the wing.

4 As you run, try to take a look up at the wing to see that it is fully inflated. This is not easy.

5 After perhaps a dozen steps, apply about a quarter of the available brake travel as you keep running. You will slow down and the wing will feel as if it really wants to fly. If you had been practising on a hillside you would now have taken off!

Getting centred

Many beginners find that the wing strays off to one side when they pull it up. This is usually because the wall is not exactly at 90 degrees to the wind, or the pilot is not in line with the centre of it, or both. A little time spent getting it right before the pull-up will save many failed attempts.

First, if your wing does not have a centre marker on its undersurface, attach one yourself. A small patch of self-adhesive sailcloth or tape stuck on the centre panel just behind the leading edge is all that is needed. Most gliders now come with such a marker, and I am surprised that they all don't. Checking that you are in line with the marker before pull-up will soon become second nature.

With helmet on and the wind coming from behind you, it is difficult to gauge its direction completely accurately. Before you start to build your wall, throw a few blades of grass or a little dust to check the wind direction.

When the wall is formed, watch the wingtips carefully. If one is tending to curl inwards from time to time, try moving towards it a little while cautiously pulling all the risers on the other side. Re-stabilise the wall and check the tips again.

Troubleshooting Don't go for a drag

If you have gauged the wind wrongly and it is stronger than you bargained for, you can easily find yourself in danger of being dragged off your feet and down the field. There is a cure for this: let go of everything except the C-risers, and heave them towards you. The wing will thrash around a lot, but it won't go anywhere.

If you pull the wing up and it tends to go off to one side, run quickly to get directly under it again. Trying to pull it above you won't work, but running under it will.

Forward launch practice

In paragliding training books it is usual to meet the forward launch before the reverse launch. This is because the training schools find that it is the easiest way of getting new pupils into the air for their first few flights, and there is nothing like a flight or two to build enthusiasm. And, of course, in Alpine countries most early flying is done in nil-wind conditions. Fair enough, but for paramotoring in Britain the skills of the reverse launch will be so useful to you that I like to keep the emphasis on it. However, there will be days of nil-wind or just the lightest breeze, when the forward launch will be the only way to leave the ground, so here it is.

Start by making sure that there really is no wind. A stake with a couple of paper streamers on it will be a help. The difference between trying to inflate a wing into a drift of 2–3 kph compared with the same drift coming from behind can be truly remarkable. If it really is calm, take a good look at the field and position your start point to take advantage of any down-slope there may be.

Lay the wing out on its back, with the lines extended over the trailing edge. Check that there are no tangles and snags, then move both the tips forward about a metre so that the wing forms a very shallow horseshoe on the ground. Attach the harness (making sure that it is facing the right way – don't laugh, it happens) and clip yourself in. The reason for bringing the tips forward is so that the wing will inflate from the middle outwards – much more stable than the other way round.

Forward launch

54

You should now be facing the direction you are planning to fly, with the wing behind you. Now reach *under and around* all the risers on each side, and take a brake handle and an A-riser in each hand. Hold the A-risers where the lines connect and spread your arms out at about 45 degrees. Note that the 'B's and 'C's should be passing back over your forearms, unobstructed. Now, get centred: move forwards very gently until you just feel the pull of the 'A's on the canopy. Shuffle into the position where you can sense that the tension on each side is equal. When satisfied:

1 Take one step back towards the wing, confident that when you surge forwards there is no reason why it will not come up absolutely squarely.

2 When you are ready, go! Set off firmly and powerfully. The aim is to put energy into the wing, rather than snatch at it. Keep the effort on: although you guide the A-lines upwards as the wing climbs overhead, don't hang onto them. The real energy comes from your shoulders pushing into the harness, not from your arms, and I like to open my hands once the launch is under way.

3 Once the wing has come up through about two-thirds of its arc, you may need to hesitate briefly to let it come fully overhead before accelerating again to get enough speed for take-off. This is very difficult to judge at first, and there is no substitute for practice.

4 Your instructor will tell you to look up at the wing as you run, to check that it is correctly inflated; this is quite difficult, especially on an uneven surface.

5 If you sense the wing moving to one side, go in that direction too so that you remain under its centre.

6 You also need to keep the brakes off as you accelerate, applying them evenly at just the right moment when the lift-off point arrives. It is depressingly easy to forget some of this at first.

MASTERING THE WING

Collision avoidance

Before venturing into the air at all, you must know what to do if there is the slightest chance of collision with another aircraft: **you must give way**.

- Approaching aircraft: both break right.

- Converging aircraft: give way to the aircraft on your right.

- Overtaking: pass on the right.

- Landing: the lower aircraft has priority.

See Figure 16 on page 140.

This forward launch is often also called the alpine launch. Some pilots seem to take to it instinctively while others struggle every time. In Britain we normally find some wind, so we tend to be more nervous of alpine launches than pilots from calmer climes. Care in laying out the wing to start with helps a lot, but there is also no doubt that some gliders have much better characteristics for it than others. This is something which manufacturers have improved throughout the years, and is a good reason for buying a recent model if you can possibly afford it.

Getting airborne

Compared with the preparatory effort, taking off with a paraglider is simplicity itself. Assuming you are launching from a hillside, it is just a matter of applying a little brake when the airspeed is high enough, and off you go. If the wind is straight on to the hill and more than about 8 mph (13 kph) you will find that it is much easier to fly than to remain on the ground. Once flying, it is good practice to let the brakes off again so that you have plenty of speed for manoeuvring.

The most common error beginners make is to 'sit down' into the seat as soon as they feel it beginning to lift at all. Resist the temptation: you will only sink to the ground and provide bum-skidding entertainment for everybody else. Keep running throughout the launch until you are hauled off the ground.

Straight flight

Unless your paraglider is trimmed very badly, straight flight should simply be a matter of keeping just the slightest even tension on the brake lines and concentrating on sitting comfortably in the harness. Try to develop the habit of crossing your legs at the ankles while cruising. This may not affect your flying but it somehow seems a bit of a confidence-booster.

Turning

The primary method of turning is by pulling the brake on the side you wish to turn to. This slows down that wing so that the other one 'flies around it'. The main thing to remember is to let the brake back up as you complete your turn. If you don't, there is a real possibility that after a short series of turns you will have run out of brake travel on both sides, while also slowing the wing so much that there is a danger of stalling it and dropping out of the sky.

You can assist the turn by leaning in the direction you want to go in. The amount to which this will help will depend on the design of the harness you are using and how tightly it is adjusted. (A slack chest strap means a greater response to weight-shift.) Once you have gained a bit of experience you will find that you are automatically co-ordinating weight and brake without thinking about it.

Try to make all the turns smoothly. The wing is virtually a part of the air and should be coaxed through it, not hauled about. This is the key to getting the best out of your glider, and it will become extra-important when you start flying with power.

Landing

The paraglider is the easiest aircraft to land. You are flying relatively slowly and have an uninterrupted view. All that is needed is to approach with the brakes almost off and then slow down so that your speed over the ground is almost nil as your feet meet it. This really is not difficult provided you set up the approach correctly.

Always approach into the wind. As soon as you have decided that you are going to land, look for clues about wind direction – flags, smoke, crops etc. Try to have your final turn completed at about 300 ft (100 m) and concentrate on the field. As the ground gets nearer, take a moment or two to check whether you are developing any sideways drift and adjust as necessary.

Keep flying at almost full speed throughout the approach. At about 100 ft (30 m), get completely

Power will make a difference
Don't get too used to using the brakes to take off. When you switch to motoring, you will have to learn to leave the brakes off and let full power take you up.

upright in the harness, with your weight on the leg-straps rather than on the seat. Keep your airspeed up. If the headwind is slight you will feel that you are going a bit too fast, but have faith!

At little more than 3 ft (1 m) above the ground, flare firmly with both brakes simultaneously. You will stop in a couple of paces, with the wing sinking to the ground behind you. If you think there is a chance of the wing overshooting, just keep running until you are sure it is down behind you.

If the headwind is more than a few miles per hour, your descent will be almost vertical and you will need virtually no flare.

Always fly fast until the final flare. If you try and slow the approach too much the glider will respond badly and there is a chance that you may stall it or spin it. Also, there will not be enough energy in the wing for it to respond properly to the flare when you want it.

As a potential paramotor pilot, you need to practise landings until you are really confident. This is because a bad landing which is simply undignified without a motor on your back may be really dangerous and expensive when power gets involved.

Collapsing the wing after landing

If your landing has gone according to plan, the wing will land behind you with the lines outstretched. In light wind there is no more to do than unclip and pack it away. If there is a breeze blowing you have to be ready for it and take immediate action to avoid being dragged backwards. On touchdown, turn immediately to face the wing and take a couple of fast steps to slacken all the lines. That will usually do the trick, with the wing settling on its back.

Opposite *Touchdown at tick-over. There is a light headwind, so the pilot only needs to make a gentle flare.*

If you have been really caught out and find yourself setting up for a landing in a strong wind, be ready to turn and pull the C-risers powerfully the moment you

touch down. Identify the 'C's during the final part of the approach, so that you are prepared. Once properly down, you can haul the wing towards you by pulling in all the C-lines. The thing to avoid is permitting the A-lines to go tight again while you are still clipped in: you will be dragged off your feet and down the field remarkably quickly.

Ridge soaring

Having learned to launch and land reliably, you will probably want to have a go at soaring before getting fully committed to powering your paraglider. By soaring we mean extending the glide by seeking out rising air and remaining in it. In Britain you usually start by flying in ridge lift at the front of hills. A breeze of 8 mph (13 kph) or so blowing onto the face of a steep ridge will be sufficient to keep you up indefinitely if you fly accurately. Apart from being one of the most pleasant ways imaginable of spending an afternoon, you will also be learning to handle the wing in a relaxed and instinctive manner.

If you are doing your learning in a land of high mountains, the emphasis will not be so much on pure ridge lift, but rather on gradually introducing you to thermal lift caused by warmed air rising as the sun heats the ground through the day. Thermal lift is also an important part of paragliding in Britain (and is described on page 61), but because this is a country of low hills and high winds, ridge soaring in the lift at the front of a hill is the usual way to start.

Assuming the wind is coming straight in, soaring is a straightforward matter of turning 90 degrees shortly after take-off and then heading parallel to the edge of the ridge for some distance before making a 180-degree turn back, and so on. Well, that is what it is like in an ideal world. In practice, the wind is not often completely square on to the slope, nor are all hills straight and regular, so there are always adjustments to be made. Also, you actually have to turn through a bit more than 180 degrees at the end of each beat to avoid gradually moving out from the hill and losing the lift. This means having to fly slightly towards the hill after the turns, and a lot of new pilots find this rather unnerving.

Active piloting

Once your flying reaches the stage where you are spending real time in the air, rather than just gentle glides in calm conditions under supervision, you should begin to learn how to feel through the brakes and harness what the wing is doing.

It is mainly a matter of lightness of touch. When you start flying you want to grip the brake handles tightly all the time to feel secure, but as time goes on you begin to relax. Above you, the pressure in the cells in the wing is constantly changing slightly in response to any shifts in wind speed and direction. The active pilot responds to these changes by making small changes to the tension on the brakes, with the object of keeping the pressure as constant as possible across the wing. In light conditions the movements will be slight, and often the effort used is little more than the weight of your hand.

With further experience you will meet stronger gusts – perhaps due to thermal activity. The active flying response is to use the controls to keep the internal pressure as constant as possible by using the brakes independently and to dampen any surges by using them both together.

A sense of active piloting will serve you well when you graduate to flying under power. You will find that you will react instinctively to such challenges as changes in trim when the throttle is opened or closed.

Thermal soaring

As mentioned earlier, thermals are a source of lift which makes long-distance flying possible in gliders of all types. Think of thermals as columns of warmed air which can be rising faster than your glider normally sinks. If you are crafty enough to stay in one you can climb thousands of feet before gliding on to find another, and so on.

For the new pilot, thermals can be a mixed blessing. The main problem is that there is inevitably some associated turbulence, plus lots of sinking air around the rising stuff.

Your first encounters will probably come when you are ridge soaring: you may feel the wing hesitate and then you will surge upwards quite fast. Just as you are beginning to quite like the sensation, the wing will feel as if it is shooting ahead and you will soon be down to your starting level again. What has happened is that you have flown into one side of a thermal, straight across the middle and then out of the other side. An experienced pilot might have been able to turn quite tightly in the rising part and climb away from the hill. However, you should simply have used your growing active-piloting skills to keep the surges of the wing to a minimum.

Exploiting thermals is a big subject. Many paramotor pilots simply look upon thermals as a source of turbulence and go to great lengths to avoid them. This is a shame, because these sources of free lift can be a big help on cross-country flights, so don't rule them out too soon.

See Chapter 13 for much more about using thermals in your flying.

Rapid-descent techniques

When you are learning, all your flying should be done in easy conditions and you should never need to use these rapid-descent techniques. However, you do need to know what people are talking about, and maybe one day you will need them. They are used mainly to escape from being sucked up into cloud due to excessive lift, but 'big ears' can also be used by hill fliers who are in danger of being blown over the back if they have misjudged the wind speed above the hill. These techniques are mainly for use when gliding: in a motor harness it may not be possible to reach the lines to pull the ears in or do a B-line stall.

Big ears

Reach up with both hands and hook a finger or two around the extreme outer A-line on each side. Then pull the lines down until the tips fold down and backwards. They will flap around a bit, but the glider will still remain completely stable. You won't be able to use the brakes while the ears are in, so all steering must be by weight-shift. That alone is good reason not to 'pull the ears' too close to the ground or other aircraft.

On most models the tips will re-inflate automatically as soon as you release the lines. It is a good idea to watch them throughout the re-inflation. If one hesitates, a steady pull on the corresponding brake will immediately cure it. I used to worry about one tip remaining stuck in, but it is not a problem – the wing does not go into a spin and it is easy to keep flying straight. In fact some instructors now recommend letting the ears out one at a time because the trim changes are more gentle that way.

In still air, pulling the big ears generally increases the rate of descent from about 220 ft/min to 350 ft/min. Because the area of wing supporting you is effectively reduced, the wing loading increases and so does the stall speed.

B-line stall

Do not do this unless you are being sucked up into a huge black cloud and have run out of other ideas. Do not even think of trying it to see what it feels like. The technique is simple: grab hold of the B-risers as near the top as you can, and haul down on both of them together. It takes a lot of effort, but eventually the wing develops a huge pleat across its span and descends vertically. Expect a sink rate of at least 600 ft/min and probably more.

To return to normal flight, simply release the risers. The wing should surge and then resume its normal forward speed. However, there is a slight risk – especially if you have released the risers slowly – that it will re-inflate fully but remain in a stalled fast-vertical-descent mode. I have never experienced this, but I am told that pushing hard on the A-risers may get it going forwards again. The other cure is more radical: it involves using the brakes to turn the stable stall into an unstable one, waiting for the inevitable surge forwards from the wing and then damping that out to complete the recovery.

It's much better, I feel, to restrict your flying to milder conditions and leave the B-lines alone.

Spiral dive

Just by steadily and progressively pulling one brake, the resultant turn will soon develop into a spiral if you keep the pressure on. This will result in rapid loss of height. It can also result in rapid pilot disorientation. The speeds can soon feel quite astonishing, and you may feel an instinct to try to stop it quickly. Resist the instinct! The way to stop a spiral is by *gradually* reducing the brake, applying opposite weightshift and very steadily flying out of it. The object is to lose the surplus speed steadily. Any attempts to reverse things by applying the opposite brake hard will have you swinging up under a surging wing.

The rate of descent in an extreme spiral can reach 2000 ft/min.

Reserve parachute

Most serious paraglider pilots are used to flying with a reserve parachute, and when they transfer to paramotoring, they naturally feel more comfortable if they can continue to carry one. On the other hand, pilots who go directly into paramotoring tend to fly in more conservative conditions and are generally content with just the main canopy. With the increasing interest in power-assisted thermal and cross-country flying, I believe we shall see more and more paramotors fitted with reserves. Although we talk of a 'reserve chute', it should be looked at as a complete system comprising the outer container (fitted to the frame or harness), bridle, deployment bag and canopy. There are many variations, but here we look at the simplest version.

How it works

You do not jump out of a paramotor if it looks as if it is going to stop flying the right way up. You remain strapped in and throw the reserve, which then lowers you and your aircraft together. The canopy is attached to a webbing bridle shaped like an inverted 'Y'. The legs of the 'Y' attach permanently to the shoulders of your harness, and the whole thing is short enough to ensure that the reserve will open below the main canopy. The system is designed to maximise the likelihood of the chute opening fully without becoming entangled with you or your probably partially inflated wing.

The canopy and its lines, all attached to the bridle, are first packed into a deployment bag and secured with an elastic loop. This is in turn packed into the outer container, with a handle (sewn to the deployment bag) protruding. A pin attached to this handle holds everything in place.

To throw the chute, you grab the handle and pull, keeping hold of it. The pin withdraws, allowing the container to open and leaving you holding the reserve in its deployment bag, which you then throw as powerfully as possible into clear air. As soon as the bridle is fully extended, it pulls free of the elastic, the deployment bag flies off and the canopy opens with a 'whump' a second or so later.

Wherever the webbing of the bridle attaches to the harness, the connection should be via metal maillons or D-rings. Never loop nylon to nylon, because in certain circumstances during the shock of inflation, friction at the junction can raise the temperature enough to cause failure.

MASTERING THE WING

Above *A reserve parachute packed into its deployment bag. You can see how the bag will fall away immediately the lines pull free of the elastic loop.*

Right *The brightly coloured package on this Revolution outfit contains the reserve parachute.*

Size is everything

Reserves come in several shapes and many sizes. Style and fashion are irrelevant: what you need is a descent rate of 5.5 metres/second or less. Bearing in mind that you have to add the weight of your motor and fuel, it is quite possible that an existing paragliding reserve will be too small. Check with your dealer, or with the BHPA, who issue an excellent guide to all types of backup chutes. Always err on the large side if in any doubt, and remember that even the best reserve will give an arrival roughly equivalent to jumping off the top of a pillar box; not an exercise to be undertaken lightly with a paramotor on your back.

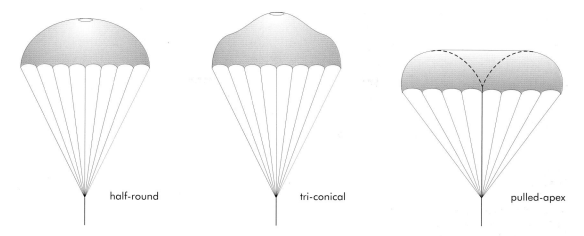

| half-round | tri-conical | pulled-apex |

Shapes

There are three main types of canopy: half-round, tri-conical and pulled-apex. The half-round is simple, but it needs to be larger than either of the others to produce the same descent rate. The tri-conical is a smart version of the half-round, and possibly my favourite. The pulled-apex is really a half-round with an extra line going straight up the middle to pull the apex down level with the periphery. These are the smallest and open fastest, but they are not as stable during descent and are relatively awkward to re-pack. Frankly, getting one big enough is much more important than what type it is; I'd be happy with any.

Where to fit it

The outer container must be fitted where the deployment handle can be located and grasped with ease. The normal positions are low on the chest or beside one of your hips. The chest position has the advantage that it can be operated with either hand, but it tends to get in the way of instruments and map-holders. The bridle must be carefully routed so that it will not strangle you when the chute is thrown. It is also most important that the outer container is very strongly attached, regardless of its position, and that the deployment handle can't be accidentally hooked by anything during normal operation. Any installation should be checked by an experienced rigger with a thoroughly suspicious eye.

Because there is such diversity in harness design, virtually every installation is a one-off. This means that there is plenty of scope for getting it wrong, so look at any installation with a sceptical eye and learn to spot possible faults. Here are a few:

- The bridle was routed so that it passed under webbing for a pulley on a speed system. The pilot would have been inverted quite remarkably violently if the chute had been used, and would have been lucky even to stay in the harness.

- The bridle was routed so that the pilot's neck would have been jammed against the top rail of the paramotor frame, which in turn would have worked like a hangman's knot.

- A chest-mounted container was so narrow that it pulled the paraglider's risers closer together, thus reducing the stability of the main canopy.

- The handle was so badly stitched onto the deployment bag that it came away with a good pull, leaving everything else neatly packed up (a popular one, this).

- Locking pins of the wrong type were used, allowing them to be pushed completely through the loops on the outer container. This guarantees that the chute will not open, regardless of how hard the pilot pulls.

That list is far from complete and new variations are discovered at every club re-packing session.

The BHPA publishes a comprehensive fact sheet about emergency parachute systems, which is highly recommended.

When to use the reserve

Throwing the chute is not something to do for fun. Your arrival back on earth will at best be disorganised and may be far worse. Even with the sophisticated 'two-riser' reserves you will be able to do little more than control the way you are facing, and if there is any wind blowing you will be going with it. The most probable reason to throw is when the wing has developed a serious spin following a partial stall and associated deflation. In this state the brake lines wrap around the risers as they all twist together, and there is little chance of recovery.

It is nice to have something positive to do at a time of crisis, and there are two 'musts' if ever you find yourself making a deployment in anger:

- Kill the motor first

- Try to haul in the wing once the reserve has opened, so that it cannot rotate around it.

Landing
The normal advice given to anyone facing the prospect of a hard landing under any type of canopy is to perform a 'parachute landing fall' (PLF). This involves hitting the ground with legs together and knees bent, and then collapsing and rolling to dissipate the energy. With a motor on your back this is unlikely to be completely effective, but nevertheless the advice to land **'legs together and knees bent'** will save much lower-limb and back damage.

The power unit

Now we get to the part where power comes onto the scene.

We spend some time here looking at the mechanical details of paramotor units because there is a large selection of different models on the market and it helps to know what you are looking at. Some of these are manufactured in quite large numbers, but others are the product of little more than backyard work-shops. It is not always easy to spot which is which, and because the industry is virtually unregulated there are no standards to guide you.

Most people coming into powered paragliding have a reasonable idea of how internal combustion engines work, maybe from experience with cars, motorcycles and mowing machines. When one of these breaks down, the result is usually little more than inconve-nience. On a paramotor it may be more serious. Although your aircraft will glide perfectly well if the motor quits, there is scope for the degree of inconve-nience to become epic; for example, when you are at 700 ft and struggling to reach the landing field against a headwind. At this point the presence of a motorway, river and railway between you and the field will con-centrate the mind wonderfully.

A minimum of about 12 bhp is needed to power an average-sized paraglider. With a suitable propeller and gearing this will be converted to a static thrust of about 40 kg. The smallest motor I have found being used commercially displaces 66 cc, but about 200 cc is common. Some motors have more than 400 cc, but these are usually designed with tandem use in mind. There is no point in having excessive power, because the aircraft cannot use it safely, and all you end up with is a machine which weighs a lot more than you need it to.

Manufacturers of paramotor units have the choice between two-stroke and four-stroke motors. They almost all choose two-strokes motors because they have a better power-to-weight ratio than similar-sized four-strokes. They are well-proven and not very expensive. However, they also have some quite strange little habits, so we'll look at them first.

Two-stroke motors

You will see from Figure 9 that the motor produces a power stroke every revolution. Now imagine that it has a capacity of 200 cc and is turning at 6000 rpm – not at all an unrealistic speed. That means that the cylinder has to gulp in and compress 200 cc of air/fuel mixture in one two-hundredth of a second, then burn it and spit the remains out in the next two-hundredth. That involves moving gases around very fast indeed, which inevitably generates lots of heat and noise. So to keep noise levels acceptable, the two-stroke needs an effective silencer for the air entering the carburettor as well as a highly efficient exhaust silencer – more about this later. It also needs extensive cooling, particularly for

Figure 9.1: Simple two-stroke cycle

[a] *Piston rising: a fresh charge of air/fuel mixture is drawn into the crankcase beneath the piston, which soon closes the exhaust port and compresses the previous charge in the combustion chamber above it.*

[b] *Ignition and combustion – the power part of the cycle. The compressed charge is burned: the piston is driven down, soon compressing the fresh mixture in the crankcase.*

[c] *and* **[d]** *Exhaust and transfer: the old charge is expelled through the exhaust port, and almost simultaneously the fresh one is pumped up the transfer passages from the crankcase into the combustion chamber ready to repeat the cycle.*

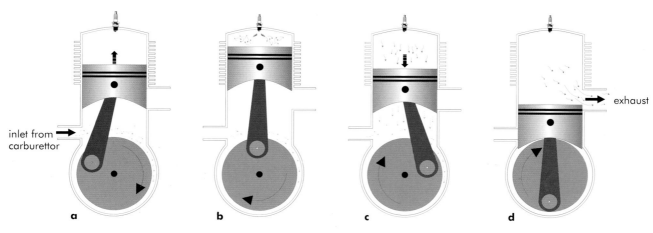

inlet from carburettor

exhaust

a   b   c   d

CHAPTER 5

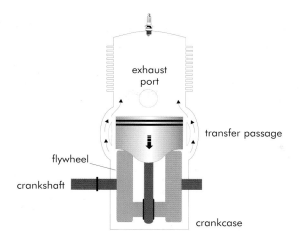

Figure 9.2: The fresh charge is pumped up from the crankcase into the combustion chamber via the transfer passages.

the cylinder and cylinder head. For this there is a choice between air cooling via aluminium fins, or a water jacket and radiator. The fins usually win, on grounds of cheapness and simplicity, even though by their resonant nature they can be a source of noise. Some of the air-cooled motors have a fan and ducting to guarantee a good flow of air around the cylinder.

The exhaust system on a two-stroke has much more to do than just conduct the gases away from the cylinder. Strange as it may seem at first sight, it is also part of the induction system. On high-performance two-strokes the exhaust pipe incorporates an expansion

The Revolution is one of the few power units to use water cooling. The black rectangle is the radiator, with its small expansion tank right at the top. The plastic pipes to the water pump show clearly. The thin red pipe is the breather from the drive gearbox, which runs up into the air intake silencer.

The Adventure F1 is about as simple as a paramotor can be. The prop runs at engine speed, driven directly from the end of the crankshaft. The motor is the air-cooled Solo 210, fitted inverted.

chamber followed by a thin tailpipe. The inlet and exhaust ports in the cylinder are allowed to remain open sufficiently long for more than a 'natural' charge of fresh mixture to enter the combustion chamber. Naturally, some of it spills out, unburned, down the exhaust pipe towards the expansion chamber. Before it travels far, it gets a very nasty surprise: it meets a shock wave travelling back up the pipe, caused by the previous burned charge meeting the restriction at the end of the expansion chamber. This has enough energy to shove much of the surplus fresh mixture back into the cylinder, providing a sort of supercharge effect.

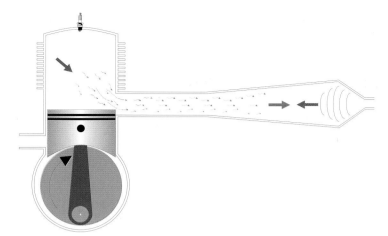

Some of the fresh charge is allowed to spill out into the exhaust where it soon meets back-pressure from the previous combustion. This has the effect of cramming it back into the combustion chamber and providing a form of super-charge. Naturally, the timing and exhaust dimensions are critical.

The efficiency of this exhaust resonance effect depends on the correct relationship of the volume of the expansion chamber, the shape and size of the restriction, and the speed of the gases. At low engine speeds the gas speeds are correspondingly low and the back-pressure insufficient to help. It is extremely difficult to provide a system of carburation and ignition timing which can cope with this, which explains why two-strokes have notoriously uneven tick-overs.

Unfortunately, the requirement for extensive induction and exhaust systems on two-strokes does rather detract from their original glorious simplicity, and makes them generally rather bulky and difficult to install. Some models do not attempt to produce very high efficiency from the motor, and consequently can use quite a compact silencer. This can be a good compromise.

Another idiosyncrasy of the two-stroke is the way in which it is lubricated: generally, its oil is mixed with the petrol. This is because the fuel has to pass into the crankcase before being pumped up into the cylinder. If raw petrol were to be used, it would soon dilute any oil lubricating the crankshaft. Instead, 'petroil' mixture is inhaled through the carburettor and into the crankcase, where enough of the oil separates out to lubricate the main bearings, the big-end, etc. These bearings are always of the ball or roller type, which

Right *Take time to mix the oil completely. Here a small quantity of fuel and oil has been pre-mixed in the jug before being added to the rest in the can and given a shake for a minute or so. Everybody has a pet way of mixing, and the main thing is always to be clean and thorough.*

Below *Adventure paramotors remind the pilot to take oil-mixing seriously.*

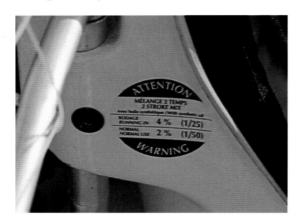

function in an oily mist, rather than demanding a pressure feed. One or two motors use a separate oil supply, in which the oil is sucked into the crankcase through an automatic valve from a small tank. Regardless of the details, all the two-strokes use their oil in the 'total-loss' manner.

Although the introduction of modern synthetic oils allows some motors to operate with an oil content of as little as 2 percent of the fuel by volume, some of the oil inevitably passes right through the motor and becomes carbon or sticky residue in the exhaust. Yet more is blown back through the carburettor (especially at tick-over), so two-strokes tend to be rather messy after prolonged use.

We are spending some time on lubricating two-strokes because it is vitally important, and also a source of mystery to many. Mixing oil with the petrol is not just an unwelcome chore: it is also the cause of engine failures because either the wrong amount of oil is used or the fuel becomes contaminated through using dirty funnels. A frequent error is to be extra generous with the oil in the belief that you are being 'kind' to the motor. In fact, you are effectively lowering the quality of the petrol you are using, because the surplus oil takes the place of some of the petrol the motor thinks it is getting, and is a much less efficient fuel. The message is: 'use the type and ratio of oil which the manufacturer specifies'. Stray from that at your peril!

Note that some engine manufacturers will specify different concentrations of oil according to whether 'normal mineral' or 'synthetic' oil is used. Whichever you choose, it is good practice to stay with it and not chop and change.

The constant need for cleanliness concerning any containers, funnels, bottles etc. used for fuel and oil should be obvious. Not only will any form of grit do abrasive damage inside the motor, but it may also cause a blockage in the carburettor before it even gets there. Water is another common contaminant, getting into the system either directly or through condensation. Water can block the small fuel jets in the carburettor very easily.

When you first get your paramotor, buy a couple of fuel cans specially for it. Why two? So that you always have one with a known quantity of fresh petrol in it ready for mixing. Label the cans so that you always know which is which. If you don't use the unmixed petrol during a particular paramotoring session, pour it into your car (unless it is a diesel, of course) and buy fresh for the next outing, because modern unleaded fuels seem to lose their volatility very quickly.

The ignition system on a two-stroke lives a rather hard life because it has to provide a spark at each revolution, rather than every other time, as on a four-stroke. Various systems are used, but they usually involve a

The Solo motor

About half the paramotor units on the market use the *Solo 210* industrial motor. In its basic form, with stock carburettor and exhaust, it delivers about 14 bhp, but several manufacturers modify it to extract as much as 20 bhp.

An Adventure F3 with tuned Solo motor. The black part to the right of the motor is the exhaust expansion chamber, followed by an aluminium silencer across the bottom. All the exhaust connections are backed up with locking wire. The blue cylinder-head is a tuned item. The nuts holding the prop on should not pass a pre-flight inspection: they seem to be only finger-tight.

rotary magneto supplying high-tension current direct to the spark-plug. The timing of the spark is absolutely critical, so this is another case where the manufacturer's settings should not be altered. Similarly, the specified spark-plug type and gap setting should be strictly adhered to.

A practical consideration for designers is that it is not very important which way up a two-stroke motor is mounted. This is handy for owners too, because, assuming the fuel system has been drained, it doesn't matter if the motor is laid on its side during transportation.

To aid starting, many two-strokes have a 'decompressor valve' fitted. This reduces the cylinder compression until the motor fires for the first time, thus making it easier to turn over from standstill.

So far only single-cylinder motors have been mentioned. These are the most common by far, but there are also twin- and three-cylinder models on the market.

Four-stroke motors

Only one or two manufacturers use four-stroke motors at the time of writing, but I feel that it is a trend which may increase. It is not the amount of power they deliver that is the attraction, but rather the quality of it. Four-strokes can be tuned to deliver their power reliably over a broad range of revs, and generally are quite tolerant of large differences in ambient air temperature and pressure.

The four-stroke produces power only on every other stroke. To carry the piston up and down on the exhaust stroke, some of its energy must be stored in a hefty flywheel. Also, mechanical valves are required to control the flow of gases, instead of being able to let the piston do it all. So any four-stroke will be heavier and more complicated than a two-stroke of comparable power.

On the face of it, that would seem to rule them out for paramotor use, where portability is vital. However, four-strokes are generally easier to start than two-strokes, run on straight petrol, run cooler and tick over reliably. They do not need such a complicated exhaust system, either.

Four-strokes are lubricated with a recirculating oil system. The simple ones which are of interest to us use a 'wet sump' system in which the reservoir of oil is at the bottom of the crankcase. Such motors can only be run if they are kept the correct way up. Also, if they are not transported more or less upright, oil finds its way into parts of the motor where it is not particularly welcome in bulk, and also out onto the floor of your car, where it will not be welcome at all.

The fuel system

At its most simple, the fuel system can consist of a tank, a tap and a fuel line which feeds the carburettor by gravity. For use in the UK, the tank must be no bigger than 10 litres. In practice, most motor units carry the tank beneath the motor and draw the fuel up by using the intermittent vacuum of the crankcase. A bulb is fitted in the line to prime the system manually. A filter should also be provided. This may take the form of a filter bowl fitted to the base of the tank, or a plastic in-line type. In-line filters have to be fitted the correct way round and are usually marked with arrows showing the direction of flow.

Personally, I would prefer not to fly a paramotor which has the tank above the motor, simply because in the remote chance of an in-flight fire I would rather not have gravity fuelling the flames.

Carburettor

The carburettor is where the air and fuel are mixed in the correct proportions for combustion. It is basically a tube (the *venturi*) through which air enters the motor. Somewhere about half-way along the tube there will be a small hole through which fuel can enter the airstream. The flow of air is controlled by some form of shutter in the venturi, and the fuel by various types of automatic valve. Further features provide for slow-running adjustment and easy starting.

There are two basic types of carburettor: *float* and *diaphragm*.

In float carbs, such as the Mikuni and the DellOrto, a reservoir of fuel is maintained at the correct level by a float-controlled valve. This is the type of carburettor found on most motorcycles. Many years ago the floats were made of thin brass and frequently sprang leaks. Fortunately, fuel-proof plastic foam is now usual, which gives much less trouble. Because the float responds to gravity, float carburettors have to be kept upright if they are to function correctly. It is also as well to drain the float chamber before transporting the unit.

In diaphragm carburettors, such as the Tillotson and the Walbro, the feed is controlled by a valve operated by a diaphragm which reacts to the reduction of pressure in the inlet venturi. The valve is spring-loaded to the 'shut' position, and atmospheric pressure behind the diaphragm pushes it open. These carbs will operate at almost any angle and do not need a large reservoir of fuel.

If fed with clean fuel, carburettors rarely give trouble. Their biggest enemies are dirt and amateur mechanics.

Driving the propeller

A propeller of the size which it is convenient to use on a paramotor becomes very noisy indeed if it has to turn at much above 2500 rpm, because its tips will be approaching the speed of sound. Few motors develop enough power at such low revs, so some form of reduction-drive is usually needed. The ratio is usually somewhere between 2:1 and 4:1, according to the torque characteristics of the motor. The most usual form is to have a large pulley on the propeller driven by a small pulley on the motor via a flexible belt. The first paramotor I saw used three individual vee-belts side by side, but this arrangement has now been superseded by a single 'Poly-vee' type – in effect a number of very narrow vee-belts sharing a single backing band. They are very reliable, but it is essential that the pulleys are accurately aligned and tensioned. Check that there is effective provision for adjustment, and that the whole arrangement looks beefy enough to last.

Fuel contamination

Water is heavier than petrol, so it will collect in the bottom of the fuel tank. The pick-up end of the fuel line should extend a couple of centimetres up into the tank so that it will be above any accumulated water and dirt.

Water can be separated from petrol by filtering the fuel through a clean chamois leather.

Some models use toothed belts – often referred to as 'timing belts' – which work well but can be harsher than the vee types. Whatever sort of belt is used, alignment and tension must be maintained carefully to ensure trouble-free operation.

The small-capacity Vittorazi motors used by Revolution and certain other makers have a system of gear-reduction. These models also have a centrifugal clutch in the driveline, which prevents the gears from being damaged by load reversals at tickover. It also makes them particularly easy to start because the starter doesn't have to spin the propeller too.

The prop fits onto a hub, usually being secured with four long bolts. The flange and the face of the prop must both be clean when they are bolted together, and each blade checked to see that it is running true.

Bolting the propeller on

CHAPTER 5

The propeller

The propellers used on paramotors can have two, three or four blades and are made from wood, metal or a variety of reinforced plastics. The blades are just small revolving wings. They have an airfoil section and a fixed angle of attack.

The hub of the prop should be marked with basic information about it. Usually this will be no more than a pair of figures, e.g. 90 × 55. The first figure is the diameter (90 cm in this case), and the second is the pitch. Here it is 55 cm, which means that the blades are set at such an angle that the prop will move forwards 55 cm in one complete revolution *if there is no slip at all.* Of course, in a fluid medium such as air, there is always lots of slip, so the measurement is purely for comparative use. There may be a third figure, e.g. '20', and the letters 'LH' or 'RH'. In this case the figure indicates the diameter of the hole in the hub (in millimetres) and the letters indicate the direction of rotation.

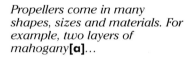

*Propellers come in many shapes, sizes and materials. For example, two layers of mahogany***[a]***…*

*…two***[b]***, three***[c]***, or even five***[d]*** layers of pine…*

…and plastic resins in a variety of shapes and colours **[e, f, g]**. *The tip of the white one shows signs of recent grass cutting. Generally, the plastic props will take a bit more abuse than wooden ones, but it doesn't do to make a habit of this sort of thing.*

The designer will have specified a prop which will be matched to the power characteristics of the motor so that both can work at efficient speeds. Because of the portable nature of paramotors, the props tend to be removed and re-fitted quite frequently, and it is very important that they are re-fitted the correct way round. More than a few pilots have found that a serious loss of performance is due to no more than having bolted the prop on so that the blades are rotating trailing-edge first.

The prop has to be fitted accurately and balanced very carefully. An unbalanced prop is not only unpleasant in flight, it will soon loosen nuts and studs on the motor and is quite capable of fatiguing its drive-shaft to the point of failure.

Figure 11: The propeller must be fitted accurately. As well as being very carefully balanced, propellers must also run true.

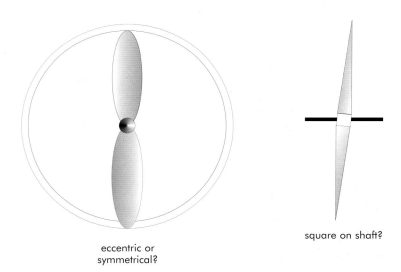

eccentric or
symmetrical?

square on shaft?

accurately balanced?

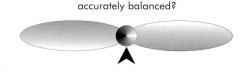

Frame and cage

The frame has to contain the motor, transmission, etc, and provide suspension points for the harness and canopy. As well as the flying stresses, it has to be robust enough to withstand the rough and tumble of everyday use. If mechanical starting is used, it will also have to put up with the loads imposed by a frustrated pilot heaving on the cord from odd angles when starting from cold on the ground. The lack of formal industry standards means that you must form your own opinion about the types of material used and the quality of the welding.

The cage will be bolted to the motor via flexible mountings which are designed to isolate it (and you) from engine vibrations. The bolts and mountings need to be inspected frequently. Watch out especially for signs of brightness where softening rubber is allowing metal-to-metal contact under certain conditions.

The main job of the cage is to keep the lines clear of the propeller at all times. It is important that the outer rim is smooth, so that the lines will slide round it easily when forward launching; and obviously the whole structure has to be strong enough for its job. The main choice is whether or not it is de-mountable for transport. If this feature is important to you, check that the ease of re-assembly matches the maker's claims. Most designs use a nylon net to 'fill the gaps' in the cage. This will do a reasonable job of keeping flapping clothing out of the prop, but not much else. It is absolutely not proof against fingers. It is worth recording in passing that several props have been destroyed because a net has not been anchored correctly.

The outer ring of the cage can be subjected to surprisingly large squeezing pressures from the lines during the early stages of a forward launch, particularly if the throttle is opened too soon. This can sometimes flex a flimsy cage enough for it to hit the prop. After a little practice you will easily know when the lines are clear and it is time to pile the power on, but until you reach that stage it is very helpful to have an instructor signalling the right moment.

A recent development has been the addition of a strong net to cover the rear of the cage (which was previously completely open). This is designed to stop slack lines from the canopy getting into the prop during failed launch attempts.

Motor controls

The controls are usually grouped together in a single unit consisting of a squeeze-throttle with a kill-button mounted on it. If there is an electric starter, the button for that will also be included. This will all be at the end of a flexible cable which must be long enough to allow no restriction when launching, yet which must not be likely to snag anywhere. A strap should be included, so that the control will stay in your hand without your having to grip it tightly all the time.

The French Adventure company produces this neat trigger-throttle unit that incorporates a dual-function instrument. When the motor is running it shows the revs, while at rest it shows total engine hours.

Sometimes a mouth-operated throttle is an option, so that the hands are free to control the glider at launch and climb-out. You change to hand-throttle once the launch drama is over. Personally, I prefer to use hand-throttle from the start; if the mechanism is well designed there is no problem managing the glider and the throttle simultaneously.

The Revolution's simple throttle. The start button is green, the kill button, red.

The kill-button is usually placed where it seems obvious that it is operated by the thumb. In spite of this, you will probably be taught to move the whole throttle unit and press the button against your helmet to stop the motor. This makes sense: your hand will be full of throttle and brake, so in an emergency it is far easier to hit a big target like your helmet, rather than fiddling about with your thumb. Having hit the kill-button, **hold it down** for three or four seconds until the motor has definitely stopped.

In addition to the kill-button, there should be a switch mounted on the frame with which to isolate the whole electrical system. When you are strapped in you won't be able to see this, but it is useful to know where it is if ever you need to reach back for it in flight – if the kill-button fails, for example. That's something to practise during a trial hang (see panel on page 27).

On motors where there is no isolator switch, some pilots fit a simple back-up consisting of a loop of cord tied around the plug cap in such a way that it can be yanked off if the motor has to be killed in a crisis: crude but effective. However, if the cord were to get wet for any reason, it could become the source of a misfire.

Running in

Most new motors need to be run in before use according to the manufacturer's schedule. Even with modern metals and synthetic oils this can be a very tedious procedure, but unfortunately it is essential. When you have just got a new unit there is an understandable desire to (a) see if it runs and (b) get it into the air. Resist such desires. Get the motor securely restrained somewhere where the noise will not disturb the neighbours, and go through the complete prescribed running-in routine.

Complete mechanical reliability

There is no such thing as complete mechanical reliability.

Motoring at last

CHAPTER
6

General motor safety

Paramotors can bite their pilots and anyone else near them. Their safe management requires a few elementary precautions which should become automatic. Think about these three headings all the time:

People – fuel – electricity

People Keep helpers, spectators and their dogs slightly forward and well to the sides before starting up. Don't be afraid of explaining where they have to go and why.

Safety note: the bystander (left) and the photographer were both standing in dangerous positions as this motor was run up. If anything had got into the prop we would have been perfectly placed to collect the pieces. The safest position is always to be forward of the power unit, like the man on the right.

Fuel Keep cans and tanks stoppered. Label the fuel tap clearly '**on**' and '**off**'.

Electricity Always assume the ignition system is live. Label the ignition switch clearly '**on**' and '**off**'. Remove the lead from the spark-plug when storing the paramotor for any length of time, or if anyone else is likely to handle it for any reason. On motors with electric starters, take particular care when re-fitting the battery after charging: it is easy to cause sparks when connecting the leads, and the chances are you have just been refuelling too …

The difference a motor makes

Apart from having power available to take you across the sky without losing height, adding a motor to a paraglider affects things in a number of different ways. You need to be aware of them all, especially if you are already an experienced paraglider pilot who decides to go motoring using the same wing.

Weight

Typical paramotor units weigh between 20 and 30 kg. Ten litres of fuel will be another 7 kg or so. Adding all this will almost certainly put your all-up weight above the recommended limit for your wing. The extra load will not be a problem as far as strength alone is concerned: the average wing in good condition will survive a load test far beyond the 6-g required for certification, so a few extra kilos won't matter too much. The extra weight will certainly raise the minimum stall speed, though, and you must expect your landing approaches to feel faster than usual. They will be.

You also need to think about the size of your backup parachute, assuming you carry one. These are very load-critical, and you will probably need to go up a size to be sure of a reasonable descent rate.

Thrust

This adds an interesting element of complexity to the basically simple paraglider, because the handling changes: the push of the power unit means that the forces working on the wing are very different from those you have been used to when just gliding.

We will have a look at what is happening to the wing first. Instead of simply having to cope with the downward force generated by gravity, it now experiences the horizontal force from the propeller as well. It receives this force in a slightly second-hand manner, via the harness and the lines. A glance at Figure 12.1 shows how the thrust affects the angle of attack of the wing. It also makes it easy to see why the forward speed is limited by the aerodynamics of the aircraft rather than by the sheer power available.

As we can see, the overall effect is more or less that the propeller drives the pilot and the pilot drags the wing. It is not hard to visualise how the wing will tend to lag behind a little when the throttle is opened initially, and how it will tend to dive forwards when power is cut (see Figure 12.2). Remember also that the torque tries to turn the aircraft, and you can imagine how it is easy to find that you are motoring away in a sort of corkscrewing roll. You can go on to make this very much worse by keeping the power on and trying to damp the effect out with the brakes.

So what is the solution? First, smooth application of power and smooth control after take-off will minimise

Figure 12.1: How the thrust affects the angle of attack

gliding (no power) – minimum drag

cruising (power on) – more drag

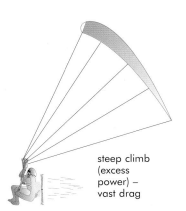

steep climb (excess power) – vast drag

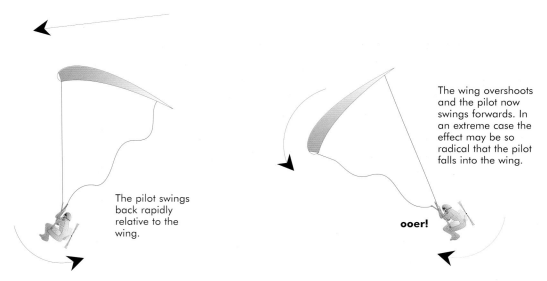

The wing overshoots and the pilot now swings forwards. In an extreme case the effect may be so radical that the pilot falls into the wing.

The pilot swings back rapidly relative to the wing.

ooer!

Figure 12.2: The effect of a sudden power cut during a steep climb

the risk of swing. If a swing develops, ease the power off to tick-over and brake very gently to stabilise the wing overhead. Leave the power off long enough for everything to settle down, make sure the brakes are right off, then re-apply power steadily.

Whenever you feel that flight is becoming unstable, the best reaction is to reduce power fairly quickly and sort the aircraft out as a glider.

Swing or oscillation under power is not unusual for your first few flights. As you gain experience you will find that your 'feel' for the wing will develop and it somehow just doesn't happen any more. While you are learning you should always use a field large enough to let you land straight ahead if you have to cut power during climb-out.

When you are starting there is a natural desire to climb as quickly as possible from take-off. If your paramotor is low on power, that may not be a bad thing, but many of them turn out more poke than the wing can comfortably handle. This can result in climbing at an artificially steep angle which can give severe pitch problems if the power cuts suddenly. If you are using a variometer and it shows a straight climb rate of more than about 300 ft per minute (1.5 m/sec), you are pushing things a bit too much.

There is an advanced technique for using surplus power to climb fast which involves putting the aircraft into a tight spiral against the direction of the torque-induced turn. This is the equivalent of a tight spiral dive in reverse and is strictly for very experienced pilots on thoroughly familiar equipment. I mention it here because I don't want a low-airtime pilot to see someone doing it and imagine that it is something to try for the fun of it.

Practical differences

If, like me, you like to paraglide in a very reclining flight position, you will probably find that the harness supplied with the motor unit prevents this. Also, the risers will attach much higher up on the harness, closer to your shoulders. This means that:

- Weightshifting your body to assist turning will not have much effect.

- The brake lines will feel 'short' and you will have to fly with your hands higher up than usual – see the panel overleaf for ways of dealing with this.

- There is more risk of stalling the wing if you are an inexperienced pilot who still flies by hand position rather than by feel.

- It may be difficult or even impossible to reach high enough to pull lines for manoeuvres such as 'big ears' (folding the tips in to increase the sink rate – see page 63). Extension cords can be attached to overcome this, but any such modifications must be checked by an expert before trying them.

- Turning round and passing the lines over your head in preparation for a reverse launch is very difficult when there is the added bulk of the cage to deal with. If you have no assistant to help, you will have to learn how to cross the risers and lay them out ready for a reverse launch before you clip in (see the photographs on page 104).

Length of brake lines

The brake handles need to be at a comfortable position in flight. If yours is a normal paraglider wing, i.e. not specifically made and set up for use with your motor harness, you will probably find that the handles are too high up for comfort when flying with power. Quite often there is sufficient extra length of line to allow the handles to be tied on a few centimetres lower down. If you decide to do this, mark the original positions on the line with an indelible felt-tip so that you can re-tie them correctly if you go back to your gliding harness. The knot to use is the bowline, which will not slip. Not a bad idea to tape the end, too.

If there is not enough line to permit re-tying, you will have to resort to fitting extensions. There are many ways of doing this, including the obvious ones of tying a short extra length of cord in, or fitting an extra pair of brake handles underneath the originals. A good solution is to fit the handles via small shackles, so that you can readily swap from 'short' to 'long' ones. Whatever you do, think of the consequences. Could the knots jam up in the guide pulleys? Will the extra handles wrap around things when launching? Have I used any links which could hook onto other lines? Have I allowed a brake line to run back out of the guide while swapping handles? Check and check again. A snagged brake can spin you into the ground.

Just how long should the lines be? If your knuckles are about level with your ears when cruising, they probably aren't far wrong. They must not be so long that you cannot flare the wing to a standstill when landing, nor so short that the full speed of the glider is not achieved.

You can check the full-speed length quite easily in flight. In smooth air, look up and look at the brake lines in detail. Note how the drag of the airstream will have put a considerable 'bow' in them; this is normal. Now observe all the attachment points on the trailing edge while pulling the brakes gently. Your hands should move at least 10 centimetres (4 in) before there is detectable movement of any part of the trailing edge.

Lastly, double-check that you have not made the lines so long that a handle will fly back into the prop if you release it in flight.

Handling

The extra weight means that your wing will be loaded more than usual and so the trim-speed will be higher. However, the extra drag of the prop and cage will make your glide angle (i.e. with the motor off) considerably steeper.

Because of the torque action, turning against the direction of rotation of the prop will be much harder than turning with it. Treat spirals in this direction with particular suspicion. Most of the power units I have come across want to turn right, but I have also flown some that rotate the other way.

This lack of symmetry means that recovery from stalls or potential spins may not be as automatic as they are when the wing is flown without power. In any situation where the wing feels as if it might be getting out of shape, cutting the power is the first thing to do. OK, there may be some curious collection of circumstances when it is not, but I can't really think of any.

When you apply power, you will move forward beneath the wing. This increases its angle of attack and, if carried to extremes, could put it close to the stall. Naturally, this effect is most pronounced when climbing under full power. For this reason, you should always climb out with the brakes off, even though your previous paragliding experience may tell you that a little brake would be appropriate.

Once under way, applying the power smoothly can make all the difference between swinging around a lot and being perfectly controlled.

Once you are flying straight and level with the brakes right off, any extra power you apply will simply make you climb. Assuming your glider has a speed bar, trimmers, or both, the way to go significantly faster is to reduce the angle of attack by pressing on the speed bar (which shortens the front risers, and pulls the front of the wing down) or letting off the trimmers (which lengthens the back risers, with a similar overall effect). You can now pile a bit more power on and cover the ground more quickly. So far, so good, but there is a hidden snag. If, on the new power setting, you suddenly let the speed bar off – an instinctive reaction if you suddenly hit rough air – the wing will immediately assume an excessively high angle of attack and there is a danger of its getting near to a stall. This is not what you had in mind, especially in rough air. The answer is to educate yourself to reduce power smoothly before releasing the speed bar.

The pilot is applying a lot of left brake here to make a tight left turn. The pilot is very experienced and knows the outfit well. Beginners should avoid braking as hard as this. The wing is Adventure's own, designed for power use but also effective just as a glider.

Torque reaction

If left to their own devices when under power, paramotors do not fly in straight lines. This is because when the propeller spins, it would really like to turn the motor around too, along with everything attached to it, including the pilot. Naturally, there is sufficient mass to prevent this, but a significant torque is experienced. This is transmitted through the harness to the wing and has a similar effect to that of the pilot permanently weightshifting to one side.

There is only one way to counteract this completely, and that is by using contra-rotating props. One Spanish design actually does this, but it needs twin engines to achieve it, so is inevitably rather complicated. However, there are various simpler ways of trimming out the torque effect. These boil down to, in effect, shortening the riser on the side away from the turn, so that there is a permanent weightshift resisting it. Of course, as soon as the power is cut, the aircraft then wants to turn the other way.

The crudest method is to add an extra karabiner where the riser attaches to the harness on the turn side. This is dangerous and not recommended at all. Some harnesses use a diagonal strap which runs from the seat on the side of the turn to the shoulder on the other side. This has the effect of transferring weight, and, if fitted with a friction buckle, can be adjusted in flight to match the power setting. This is a neat compromise. One or two designers make the frames of the paramotor unit itself asymmetric, to produce a similar effect.

Fastening the diagonal strap. This can be adjusted in flight to offset the turning effect of drive torque. Not all harnesses have a diagonal strap.

Any asymmetric alterations to the gliding trim will affect the way the wing will recover from deflations. This will not be a problem if you use a wing which has a good reputation for solid stability, e.g. DHV 1–2 rated, but could increase the risk of entering a spin on a very sensitive one.

Precession

People frequently confuse torque reaction with precession, but the two are quite different. Precession is the tendency of a rotating mass to want to turn at right angles to an imposed direction of turn. The classic demonstration which most people recall is that of spinning a bicycle wheel and feeling it respond to your efforts to turn the spindle sideways.

I am convinced that the substantial rotating mass of the propeller must behave as a gyroscope, but I confess that in flight I have been unable to detect it. However, I am prepared to believe that in turbulent conditions precession may become a complicating factor. I am unclear about whether it would emerge among the forces of good or evil in such circumstances.

Wake turbulence

When your paramotor is flying, there will inevitably be a wake of turbulent air behind it. This comes from three main sources: the stirring-up caused by the aircraft's general shape and speed (related to profile drag); the spirals of air generated at the wingtips by the pressure differential above and below the wing (related to induced drag); and the prop-wash.

This disturbance can persist for many seconds. You need to keep it in mind when flying in the company of other paramotors, particularly if you fly close behind one. It is typically experienced as almost a 'thump' on your wing, accompanied by a height loss of a foot or two. The first times you meet it, you may imagine that you are falling out of the sky, and will be a little disappointed to discover that the encounter was undetectable to ground observers. On a wing with good stability there will be no drama and the disturbance will be over before you need to do anything. Others may need, at most, a little pitch-dampening with the brakes. You soon learn to anticipate it and to discount it when it happens.

The ability of wake turbulence to persist can be the source of surprises when you start to practise tightening your turns. You will discover that you have the privilege of flying through your own wake. That can concentrate the mind wonderfully for a second or two. The effect is most noticeable in calm air, because the turbulence is dispersed more quickly if there is some wind.

The only time you really need to take wake turbulence into account seriously is when landing. You don't want to be affected by it very close to the ground, so always keep good separation when sharing a landing field.

Pre-flight inspection

Pre-flight inspection has to become a way of life for any pilot. Potential problems *have* to be found while you are still on the ground, for everyone's safety.

Checks of the wing were dealt with in Chapter 4; here we look at the entire motor unit. When you got your paramotor, these routines should have been covered in its manual. If this is the case, let me stress that what is written here does not take precedence over the maker's recommendations. However, manuals do get lost and this approach is fairly reliable.

You will need to move the propeller during the inspection, so I prefer to do it with the spark-plug cap removed.

Vibration often results in paramotor exhaust systems destroying themselves. The signs of fresh brazing on this silencer are by no means unusual. Depending on the design of the system and its mountings, it is often worthwhile to fit a restraining wire to stop any parts swivelling into the prop in the event of failure. Pick up the first signs of failure during your pre-flight check.

The general principle is to break the items for inspection down into logical groups, and then to go through each group systematically. As each group links to another, this will ensure that the whole lot is covered automatically by the end of the routine. Here are the groups:

Frame, cage and attachments: Inspect all the tubing. Look for bending and for cracks in welds at stress points. Check for tightness all bolts, pins, clips etc holding it together. Check the net.

Harness: Inspect all attachments, torque arms etc.

Motor: Work through logically, from inlet to exhaust. Start at the air filter (famous for coming adrift – fit a safety wire), then the carburettor, throttle-cable attachments etc, cylinder, crankcase, exhaust. Look for any signs of loose bolts. Pay extra-special attention to the exhaust, checking for cracks in the pipe or silencer and for rubber mountings starting to break up.

Drive: Check the belt adjustment and inspect for wear at edges. If possible, check that both pulleys are tight.

Propeller: Check that the securing bolts are tight – be particularly scrupulous about this if you have a bolted-up three-blader. Inspect the blades closely, especially if wooden, for nicks and splits. Check tip/cage clearance at several points.

Fuel system: Start at the tank and work through to the carburettor. Check that fuel is adequate, the cap secure, the vent-airway clear. Check that the tap is open (if fitted), clips firm, no signs of splitting in pipes, filter clean, carb attachment tight. Prime the system, eliminate bubbles, check throughout for leaks.

Control system: Check for kinks in the flexible cable. Operate the throttle over its full range to see that it closes easily when released.

Electrical system: Check that the master switch is **off**. Make a visual check of all wiring, looking particularly to find chafing or fraying where it passes close to other components. Check that the battery is secure (when fitted). Inspect the HT lead to the plug: it must be dry and clean. Finally, re-fit the plug cap and feel that it clicks on firmly. Switch the master switch **on**.

Yourself: Make sure that you have absolutely no loose item such as straps, scarves, drawstrings or even long hair which could find its way into the prop or reduction drive.

Your paramotor is now ready to be warmed up.

Once you have become familiar with your machine, you will find that you can conduct the whole process in less time than it takes to read about it. Do make a point of doing it without being interrupted. Nobody will mind being asked to wait a little until you complete the pre-flight routine.

You can make life easier for yourself by wire-locking many of the critical nuts. Others can be 'spotted' after being correctly tightened by dabbing them with engineers' marker paint and scribing a line across the join (Tipp-Ex will do very well, too).

Of course, too much familiarity soon breeds contempt, and it is easy to think of some particular part you have previously checked fifty times 'oh, that never comes loose' and start to overlook it. It may only need a small change in the vibration frequency – set up by a chip out of the prop, for example – to slacken it.

I tend to go on a bit about safety and propellers. More than any other aircraft, paramotors have the potential to bring people and propellers together. That is such a dangerous combination that a little paranoia in this department does no harm. For example, because an ignition switch is off, don't assume the motor cannot start. Most of the motors I know of use a magneto of some type to supply the spark. These are isolated by earthing them. It can need only a bad earth for the system to go live even though the switch is off. Consequently, as far as I am concerned, the only really safe motor is one with the plug lead(s) off.

Another danger feature is that you can walk about and turn round quickly with the motor ticking over on your back. The public, especially youngsters, may simply not recognise the danger and get too close. Even at tick-over the prop tips will be running at amputation speed, so whenever you start up, first have a really good look round through 360 degrees and shout '**clear prop**' loud enough to let anybody know that you really mean it.

I had imagined that the worst a hot exhaust could do to a careless pilot would be to inflict burns on the flesh if the pipe were touched. That was until I heard of an incident in which the risers were allowed to lie against an exhaust which promptly melted them substantially. Unfortunately, this was not noticed until shortly after take-off, when the lot parted.

Finally, whenever two or more paramotor pilots are operating together in the same field, agree a live area and a dead area and don't allow any motors to be run in the dead area.

Warm-up

Warming up the motor is essential before taking off. This is the time to discover whether you really did eliminate all the bubbles from the fuel line. The exact routine should be stated in the motor's manual, but generally you should take two or three minutes gradually building the revs up before trying a short burst of full power.

Even if the motor is already warm, it should be warmed up before each take-off.

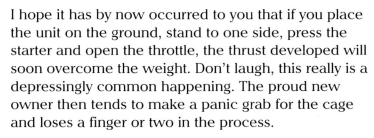

If there is someone to help, full-power tests after warming up can be performed safely. Generally, you shouldn't rush to get the motor warm enough to take full throttle, but nor should you keep it on a very slow tickover for too long either. About 3000–4000 rpm will be about right for most two-strokes.

I hope it has by now occurred to you that if you place the unit on the ground, stand to one side, press the starter and open the throttle, the thrust developed will soon overcome the weight. Don't laugh, this really is a depressingly common happening. The proud new owner then tends to make a panic grab for the cage and loses a finger or two in the process.

The paramotor has to be anchored when running, and the most usual way is to strap it to you, the pilot, who then has to provide the necessary resistance. A properly briefed helper pushing against your shoulders is as good a way as any, but if you are alone you can brace yourself against a solid object such as the side of a car. Another way is to sit down with your legs out in front of you, but this method brings the prop tips very close to the ground, with the chance of them picking up grit, grass or small stones.

If you can't get the motor to run reliably without misfiring after warming up, shut it down and look for the possible causes (plug, fuel, wiring, etc). If it won't run properly on the ground it is unlikely to cure itself in the air. And if it really isn't your day it will quit completely at full blast about fifteen feet up from launch.

Preparing for a reverse launch

In Chapter 4 we dealt with doing a reverse launch with a paraglider. This involved lifting one set of risers over your head as you turned to face the wing. It is much more difficult to do this with the motor unit on your back, because often some of the lines become hung up on the cage. It's OK if you have an assistant, but on your own it can be a real trial. The solution is not to clip in at all until the wing is laid out with the risers crossed. Then you simply hook your karabiners onto the appropriate risers, and you should be ready to pull the wing up for the inflation. The trick, of course, is to know exactly which way to clip in and then which way to turn. Fortunately it's easier to do than to explain, but I'll have a go. The pictures will help. Be sure to leave some slack in all the lines until the very end of this procedure, and don't try it alone in more then a slight breeze.

1   Start with your harness on, and (if you haven't the luxury of an electric starter) the motor ticking over.

2   With the wing on its back and the trailing edge towards you, lay out the lines and risers fully.

3   Cross one set over the other.

4   Make a half-turn in the same direction with both sets and place them on the ground. The brake handles should now be uppermost.

Jolyon Harrison shows how to clip in for a reverse launch:

[a] Check that all lines are clear, A-risers uppermost.

[b] Cross left over right.

[c] Give each set of risers a half-turn to the right. This brings the brakes uppermost.

[d] Clip in, making no other adjustments.

[e] We turned the motor unit a half-turn to the right, as if launching. As you see, the lines are clear and correct.

5 Facing the trailing edge, without twisting the risers further, clip the one on your left to the left harness karabiner and join the right side similarly.

6 Note which shoulder the uppermost set of risers goes to. That is the shoulder which must move backwards when you eventually turn.

7 Take hold of the brake handles so that your left hand controls the right wing as you look at it, and vice versa.

8 Check that the brake lines run free and that you haven't managed to get a full twist in them round the risers.

9 Check that the throttle-cable is routed clear of the lines.

10 Mentally rehearse the turn.

11 Take hold of the A-risers, build the wall and get ready to go!

If you launch and discover as you climb away that you have twisted risers or a brake line routed the wrong way, don't panic. You can sort out the line when you have reached a safe height, and most wings will tolerate a twisted riser without any trouble. All you may notice is a little extra friction on the brake controls. Don't make a habit of it, though!

Reg Bradley makes a reverse take-off with his DK Whisper.

[a] *He's clipped in with the lines crossed.*

[b] *He pulls the wing overhead, checking it with the brakes.*

[c] *Now he's turned and is applying full power for the launch. The brakes are almost off now.*

Batteries

Few paramotors incorporate charging circuits, and those that do tend not to be run frequently enough to keep a battery in good order. Therefore, if yours has electric starting, you will have to look after the battery correctly and be sure that it is charged up before each day's flying. There are several types, and they need different treatment according to their chemistry. It's worth getting it right, because apart from the expense and the chance of missing some flying when yours is flat, they can be destroyed equally easily by excessive charging or by neglect.

Some batteries like to be stored fully charged, while others need to be discharged or 'cycled', i.e. steadily charged and discharged during the storage period. Find out exactly what yours needs and set up a routine to deal with it.

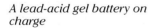

A lead-acid gel battery on charge

It is easy to become casual about handling batteries, but you should keep in mind that the chemicals they contain must be kept away from the fabrics of gliders and harnesses. Even sealed batteries can become unsealed and leak when they get old, but the worst offender is likely to be the vented lead–acid variety. Store and transport these separately from the rest of your equipment.

The big day

After some time spent learning to paraglide and getting familiar with the mechanical details of the paramotor, you will at last wake up to the day when you make your first flight. This chapter tries to give a flavour of what it will be like and what you can do to make it as effortless as possible. It is put together from my own experiences and those of several others.

At Northern Paramotors, Jolyon Harrison explains that launching is a process during which the authority moves from the pilot to the wing, then to the motor and then back to the pilot. This is a realistic way of breaking it down:

107

- *Pilot* initiates inflation

- *Wing* takes over; pilot must keep centralised under it

- *Motor* power on: pilot is dependent on motor for lift-off

- *Pilot* recovers authority for climb-out and flight.

Apart from your instructor, it is a great advantage if there are a couple of other first-timers or very-low-air-time students with you. That way, you learn from each other's experience and have time to rest between the bursts of activity. Regardless of your previous experience, you will probably be asked to do a couple of trial inflations with the motor dead. The high hang points and unfamiliar weight on your back will make these surprisingly hard work, and even very experienced paraglider pilots tend to feel like novices again.

Then you will be subjected to a little engine work: getting used to the feel of the thrust again, checking that it picks up from idling easily, and so on. This is the time to discover that the fleece gloves you decided to use, because they were nice and flexible and not too thick, also offer so little grip that the brake handle and alloy throttle keep slipping at critical moments. Thin leather gloves are the answer.

You are taken through the pre-flight checks on motor and wing, but if truth be known, you are not really taking it in properly because you are so focused on the forthcoming launch.

At last the instructor decides you are ready. The wind is very light and shifting a bit. That means a forward launch (your secret dread). Although you will have been encouraged to make your own check that the wing is overhead and fully inflated during the launch run, you will also be reassured that he (or she) will not give you the 'full throttle' signal unless all is well. You will also have been told, probably several times, that

'full throttle' for take-off means exactly that. No pussy-footing: pour on the power steadily until you are giving it the lot, then hold it there.

Dry mouth. 'Clear prop.' The motor is ticking over on your back. You give the throttle a slight squeeze to check that it will respond. The instructor walks away out into the field, sniffs the breeze, plants a wind streamer almost directly in line with you and raises both arms. No backing out now. You pace forward and lean into the harness, guiding the risers up smoothly each side, fearful that you will inadvertently catch the throttle on something and open it prematurely. No problem; the wing swings up and you see the instructor signalling you to run to the right. You go that way a little, and suddenly the wing feels fine. Immediately you get the winding-hands signal for 'full throttle' and squeeze it open, just remembering in time to keep your arms high so that the brakes stay off as you do so. Giving it full whack like this doesn't feel at all comfortable because instinct tells you that it will have you flat on your face in nanoseconds. However, this time there is the drag of the wing to help, and all that happens is that running becomes magically easy and fast for a few more paces, then the harness hauls you off the ground and you are flying!

Climb-out. At last you and your paramotor are in your element. You keep the throttle open with a death-grip for some seconds, but very soon the feeling of flight makes you feel secure – so much more reassuring than the stressed half-and-half experience of the take-off. At about a hundred feet you may just ease off a little and wriggle into the seat more comfortably. Then, still climbing, you give some thought to where you are going. You will almost certainly find that the outfit is slowly but insistently turning. You pull a little brake on the opposite side and it straightens out, but relax for a second and the turn comes back. That is the torque reaction, and dealing with it soon becomes instinctive. On most paramotors it is only really noticeable when climbing under lots of power.

Maybe there will be a little turbulence as you pass over some trees at the edge of the field. Perhaps you will throttle back in this, hesitate a second, then power-on

Below and **opposite** *A genuine first flight. Gary Eato gets his Revolution/Firebird Flame into the air for his first powered flight.*

again and find that you are swinging from side to side like a pendulum. You try to damp it with the brakes, but somehow don't seem to be able to hit the right timing and the swing gets worse. The cure is simple: power down to idle, brakes right off. The effect will soon disappear, and then you can apply throttle steadily and start climbing again. I still haven't completely mastered the art of damping this sort of swing with the power on.

Soon you will have made a circuit or two and be preparing for the landing. Don't try to be clever and land close to the edge of the field. Because of the extra weight and drag, your sink rate will be greater than you are used to as a paraglider pilot, and the glide angle will be steeper, so pick a spot with plenty of space around it. My preference is to come in with a dead engine for all the early flights, so that there is absolutely no chance of getting lines in the prop during deflation. The extra weight of the motor unit is only a problem if you come in far too fast or carelessly try to turn round to collapse the wing. Then the momentum can take you off your feet in a tragically undignified end to your first-flight triumph.

It's time for a quick de-brief, and then the next trainee is clipping in. You watch, critically, now a one-flight expert! His engine-off trials go OK, and you are sure he looks far cooler than you felt. The wing comes up beautifully and he's soon getting the power-on signal. All goes well for a few paces, but just as the power really begins to take effect he makes one of the most common errors in the book: he sits into the harness. For a long moment he sags back to earth, the propeller tip scattering grass cuttings before clawing up into the air. As he climbs away the instructor's sigh is audible.

Sitting down as soon as the harness begins to lift at all is one of the commonest mistakes, and potentially an expensive one. In this case he was lucky and there was just a little erosion to the paint on the propeller tips, but it is really easy to smash them this way. The only solution is to really educate yourself to **keep running** until you simply cannot any more because there is no ground under your feet.

The third and last pilot in your little group is just a bit too tentative when pulling up the wing on the first couple of attempts. Finally, dead determined, he puts everything into it on the third go and gets it up OK. However, he is so determined to keep the wing going forwards at any cost that he is leaning forwards and crouching as he runs. This makes the thrust-line of the motor operate at almost 45 degrees downwards, and you all have an anxious few seconds as he struggles under the load without accelerating very well. Eventually he allows himself to get more vertical in response to the instructor's frantic signalling and is off the ground in another step or two at most.

By the end of the day, theory will have become practice.

By the end of the day you will all have made three or four flights, flown circuits to right and left, gingerly tried a few 360s in either direction and made a dead-engine landing from 1000 feet. A good collection of tasks to tick off in the logbooks. During the circuits you will have begun to find time to adjust the torque strap on the harness to reduce the turn under power and to keep an eye on your vario-altimeter while flying straight and level at a chosen height. Above all, the strange launch process has begun to make sense. The control is beginning to pass effortlessly between pilot, wing, motor and back to pilot without the joins being quite so noticeable.

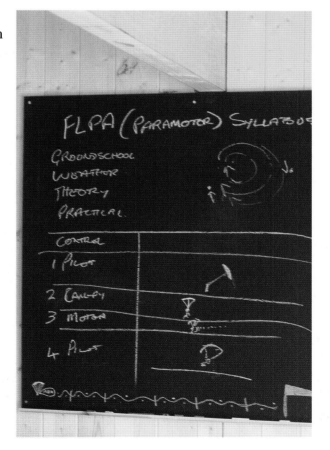

The air and the weather

When you start flying your paramotor, you will be concerned to have light winds and fairly stable air. As your experience develops you will be able to cope with more variable conditions and to exploit the free lift that is available in thermals. You will also develop an obsessive interest in the wind because it has such a profound effect on the progress you can make in a aircraft that flies at only 20 or 30 mph. In any case, the paramotor is essentially a fair-weather machine and should not be used in strong wind or rough air unless you are very experienced.

If you are already an experienced paraglider pilot, you will have acquired lots of weather knowledge. Most of this will be directly relevant to paramotoring, but there are differences. For example, by keeping the power on you will be able to fly through sink that would have put you on the ground if you were simply gliding. This gives you the opportunity to fly into corners of the sky that can be dangerous if you don't understand exactly what the weather is doing.

In my own experience, one of the most disconcerting things I discovered when I started paramotoring was just how much the wind shifts around in a completely flat field compared with its behaviour on a hill site. The hill has the effect of straightening the flow to some extent: sure, it swings a few degrees from time to time, but usually that's all. In an airfield with light winds and any local thermal activity at all, the direction can change constantly, with swings of 90 degrees quite common. This can make you feel like a novice again while launching until you learn to monitor it at very frequent intervals while taking off. A couple of strategically placed streamers or a windsock will be a great help.

This chapter describes some of the basic characteristics of weather that you need to know for your own safety and to satisfy the BHPA examiners. 'Further reading' on page 185 lists several good books which cover this vast subject in far greater detail.

Whatever your experience, develop the habit of constantly observing the weather and trying to work out what is going on. It is a huge and complex subject, so this chapter can do no more than introduce the general concept of weather systems and give an indication of how they behave.

The air

The air we fly in is the troposphere, which extends from the earth's surface up to about 40,000 ft (10 km). As a paramotor pilot you will almost certainly use no more than the bottom quarter of this. 'Tropos' is a Greek word implying 'turbulent', and the troposphere is constantly active.

Air is a mixture of gases – mainly nitrogen, but about 20 percent is oxygen and there is a small but highly significant content of water vapour.

Most of the time we take little notice of the air, and tend to think of it as weightless and invisible. Although it is indeed generally invisible, it does have considerable weight which reveals itself as pressure when we use barometers to measure it.

Naturally, this pressure is greatest at the earth's surface, because that is where there is the greatest depth of air above to produce the pressure. Therefore, the higher you fly, the lower the air pressure.

Lapse rates

As well as the air pressure dropping with height, so does the temperature. This reduction of atmospheric temperature with height is called the *adiabatic lapse rate.* Unless there are local factors affecting it, air temperature reduces with height throughout the troposphere. This happens simply because of the reduction in pressure – not because the heat is absorbed by something else. If the air is dry, the adiabatic lapse rate is approximately 3 C° per 1000 ft (1 C°/100 m). This reduces progressively according to how much water vapour is present. It drops to about half the dry rate (1.5 C° per 1000 ft) when the air is saturated, i.e. when it is holding as much water vapour as it can. You may find the terms 'DALR' and 'SALR' occurring in meteorological information: they are Dry Adiabatic Lapse Rate and Saturated Adiabatic Lapse Rate respectively.

When a lapse rate is measured at a particular place, it is referred to as the Environmental Lapse Rate (ELR) and takes into account all local factors. When this differs significantly from the expected adiabatic lapse rate there will be lots of vertical motion in the air. For more about this, see the section on thermals (page 118).

We go on about lapse rates because some knowledge of them is very useful to paramotor pilots. The ELR can indicate how much thermal activity there will be and how high cloudbase is likely to be.

Air movement

Movement in the air is primarily caused by the sun, which heats it up unevenly and, curiously, from the bottom up. The air reacts like any other gas – as it gets warmer it expands. This reduces the density, and the warmer portions of air then float upwards and cooler air flows in to take their place. The effect occurs locally, where its simplest form causes coastal breezes, and globally, where there is a persistent tendency for air to move from the Poles towards the Equator. Wind is simply the effect of air moving from areas of high pressure to areas of lower pressure.

That air heats from the bottom up is due to its transparency. The sun's rays do not heat it directly, in the same way that they do not heat a clear glass window as they pass through. However, they do heat the earth's surface underneath and that in turn transfers warmth to the air which is in direct contact with it.

Naturally this means that the air adopts the nature of the surface below, so it is easy to imagine the earth surrounded by many air masses with different characteristics. For example, cold air over the polar areas, relatively warm and damp air over the oceans, and hot, dry air over deserts. Air is fairly reluctant to mix, so the edges of different air masses are often readily identifiable. Where they do meet and one advances into another, we talk of the interface as a 'front' (see page 119).

Thermals

On a much more local scale, the tendency of the atmosphere to warm up unevenly leads to the development of upward-moving portions of air called *thermals*. On the ground, a dark-coloured or sheltered area will heat up more than a light-coloured area or one exposed to the wind. In turn, more heat is transferred to the air in contact with the warm areas until it becomes buoyant enough to break free from the surface. This 'bubble' of warm air floats upwards, and cooler surrounding air flows in to take its place. If you enter a thermal when you are flying, it will feel like a column of lift which can be quite violent. It is not unusual to climb at 1000 ft per minute in a good thermal.

Circular motion

Before we leave the topic of air movement, it is helpful to have a look at why weather systems on maps and satellite photos form great swirls, rather than long straight strips. It is all down to the fact that the world spins on its axis, and the atmosphere relies on friction and gravity to keep it all moving round with the earth at the same speed. If the air were all at the same temperature and pressure, there would be no problem, but the vertical movements allow the air masses to become sufficiently destabilised for them to be deflected by the earth's rotation. In the northern hemisphere the effect causes air to flow anticlockwise around areas of low pressure (*depressions* or *cyclones*) and clockwise round high-pressure areas (*highs* or *anticyclones*). This is called the Coriolis effect, after the French mathematician who formulated much of the theory of relative movement.

In the southern hemisphere the direction of flow is the opposite of that in the northern. Around the equator the effect is, understandably, less pronounced, so straighter air-flows are noticeable there.

Isobars

Isobars are lines linking points of equal air pressure on a weather map. By convention they are drawn at 4-millibar intervals. The closer the isobars, the stronger the wind will be. At 2000 ft the wind will generally be found to flow parallel to the isobars, whereas on the surface it will have backed by up to 30 degrees (in the northern hemisphere). This is well worth remembering when planning cross-country flights, particularly in an aircraft as slow as a paramotor.

Fronts

The following brief descriptions are based on the maritime climate of the United Kingdom and Western Europe. In areas with drier climates the effects will be less marked.

Warm front

When a warm air mass advances into cooler air, a 'warm front' forms. The warm air is less dense than the cooler air, so it tends to be forced upwards along the interface. As it climbs, it also cools, and this causes any moisture present in the form of water vapour to condense and become visible as cloud and rain.

When the front has passed, conditions will steady down and it may become quite good for paramotoring

A wind whose direction changes in a clockwise direction is said to *veer*; when it changes anti-clockwise, it *backs*.

Isobars provide a 'picture' of air pressure on a weather map by linking places where the calculated mean sea-level pressures are equal.

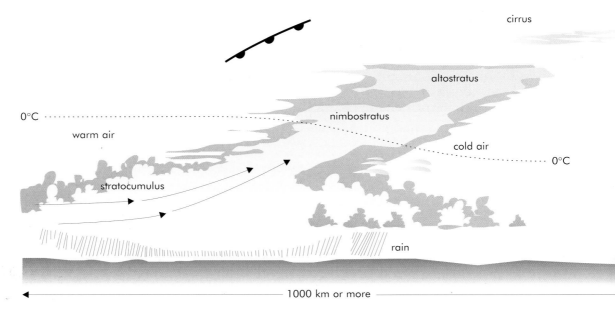

cirrus

altostratus

0°C

warm air

nimbostratus

cold air

0°C

stratocumulus

rain

◄———————————— 1000 km or more ————————————

Figure 13: Warm front advancing. This greatly simplified illustration shows the cloud types that characterise a warm front. Although we are used to seeing fronts represented by thin lines on a weather map, they are really quite broad areas of disturbance.

at a fairly low altitude, even though there will still be cloud about.

Cold front

When a cooler air mass advances against a warm one, a cold front occurs. Along this, you can think of the dense, cool air moving in under the warmer air and so easing it upwards. Again the warm air goes up, the moisture condenses, and cloud and rain are likely. As the illustrations show, a cold front forms a steeper angle than a warm one, so its passage appears faster.

Fronts and lift

As a paramotor pilot you will mainly be interested in the way fronts are associated with unstable air. 'Unstable' in this context means that the lapse rates are high, so there is likely to be thermal lift. If you are an adventurous pilot who is used to soaring, this free energy opens the door to extending your cross-country flight potential. If you just like to cruise around in quiet air with the motor keeping you going, it is not quite such good news.

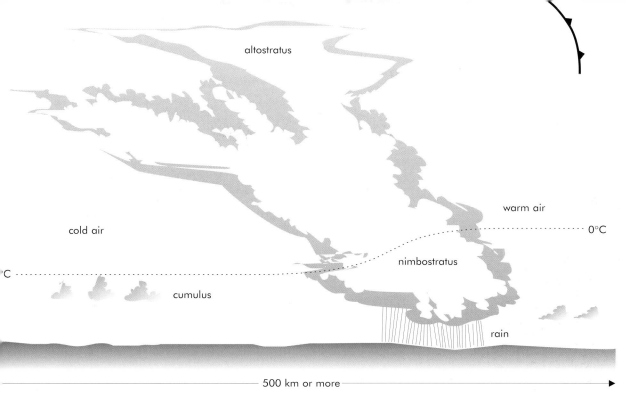

altostratus

warm air

cold air

0°C

°C

nimbostratus

cumulus

rain

500 km or more

Figure 14: Cold front advancing. Its width is far less than that of the warm front. From the ground, the altostratus clouds may conceal cumulonimbus too, if the front is particularly active. It is possible for a cold front to catch up with part of the warm front preceding it. The result is an occluded front, a sure sign that the associated depression is weakening.

Clouds

Clouds are condensed water vapour in the form of tiny droplets. They form because at any given temperature the air is capable of containing only a certain amount of invisible gaseous water vapour. The warmer the air, the more vapour it can support. When the critical amount is reached, the air is said to be *saturated*, and any surplus vapour present will condense into droplets. If this occurs at ground level the result is mist or fog; once well overhead, it is cloud.

The temperature at which the condensation happens is called the *dew point*. Bearing in mind that air cools with height (see the section on lapse rates on page 117), it is easy to appreciate why cloud forms under the right conditions and why the cloudbase is roughly at the same level on good flying days. Assuming that the sky is clear enough to allow for some solar heating, the cloudbase will normally rise throughout the day as the ground warms the air above it, which is something to bear in mind if you are a paramotor pilot with a range of hills to cross.

Wind gradient and low-level turbulence

At the levels you will be flying in, the wind speed increases with height. This is because the movement of the air closest to the ground is reduced by friction. It is very important to remember this if you are tempted to launch in wind speeds close to the top speed of your wing: you may discover that you are travelling backwards relative to the ground as soon as you have climbed a few hundred feet.

You also need to keep the wind gradient in mind when landing. This time it is the lack of wind speed which may bring the problems: you need to keep plenty of flying speed on to avoid the possibility of stalling on approach. You must also expect your relative glide angle to flatten out as the ground approaches, so always make sure that you have plenty of field to spare.

Any obstructions upwind on the ground will interfere with the airflow. Trees, houses, earthworks – anything can generate turbulence. The stronger the wind, the further the turbulence will extend. Watch out for the effect, especially when landing.

In the lee of hills you will find sinking air. It is quite possible that it may be sinking faster than you can climb, which is a very uncomfortable experience. The only safe solution is to fly out of the influence of the hill, which usually means back the way you came.

If approaching the corner of a hill from downwind, expect to meet increased wind speeds caused by the air speeding up as it flows round the end.

When you are at all close to the ground in hilly country, you can never take the direction or strength of the wind for granted. For example, imagine a valley lying more or less at 90 degrees to the wind prevailing at 2000 ft. Down below the tops of the hills you can be confident that the wind will be along the valley one way or the other, but which way? Its overall direction can change very quickly in these circumstances, perhaps being affected by strong local thermal activity or by a shift of only a few degrees in the upper wind. This effect can be very common in alpine valleys, but it also occurs in our less dramatic scenery.

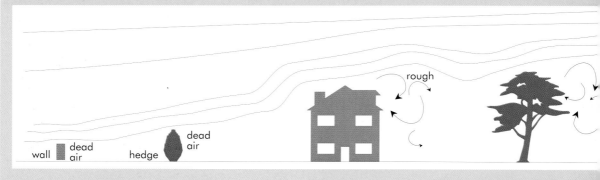

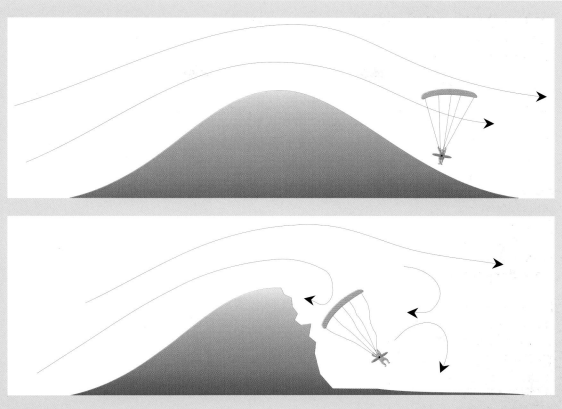

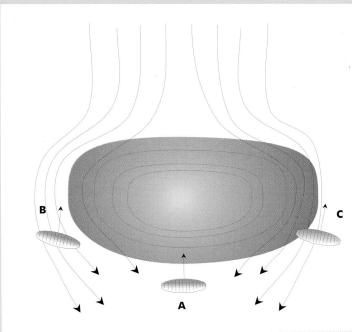

The effect that local features have on low-level wind can get you into trouble.

Figure 15.1 (**opposite**): *When landing out, any obstacles upwind can generate turbulence. Beware of walls and hedges. Although a metre or two of clearance may feel OK in nil-wind, for a really safe approach allow a clearance of five times the height of the obstacle.*

Figure 15.2 (**top**): *In the lee of hills there will, at best, be sink. There may be severe rotor turbulence.*

Figure 15.3 (**left**): *Wind will flow around a hill as well as over it. Expect sink at* **A** *and difficulty in penetrating at* **B** *and* **C**.

There are several types of cloud, categorised according to their nature and the altitude at which they are found. You know you are well on the way to being a real pilot when you can't go out of doors without mentally ticking off the clouds.

Cumulus clouds have a heaped-up appearance. At the lowest levels they are very obviously separate from one another, and even in the highest cumulus types (*cirrocumulus*) this separateness is still fairly obvious. Cumulus are good news for soaring pilots because they indicate thermal activity.

Stratus clouds appear as sheets of cloud. These sheets can vary in depth from gauze-like *cirrostratus* to the thick depressing rain-laden *nimbostratus* of a British winter.

Nimbus clouds are associated with rain.

Cumulus building into cumulus congestus

Clouds and altitude

The nature of clouds varies with the altitude at which they exist. They are grouped into high, medium and low clouds, but there can be a lot of overlap. There is also considerable variation in the heights of certain clouds according to the type of land beneath them.

High clouds are the *cirro* group. These rarely occur below 20,000 ft, and may be as high as 42,000 ft. The highest are the *cirrus*, which have the appearance of wind-blown wisps. These are sometimes called 'mares' tails'. Because the air at such altitudes is extremely cold, the cirro group are largely formed of ice crystals.

Medium-height clouds are the *alto* group. Typically these are between 7,000 ft and 20,000 ft. As well as the obviously-named *altostratus* and *altocumulus* types, *stratocumulus* lurk towards the bottom of the medium-height group.

Low-level clouds do not have a group name, but they are the ones with which you will become most familiar. *Cumulus* are the fluffy cotton-wool clumps which characterise summer days in temperate climates. Their presence marks thermal activity and the likelihood of good lift for soaring: ideal if you are paragliding, but may make the air uncomfortably bumpy if you are just starting your paramotoring career.

With a bit of encouragement, i.e. sun, humidity and a significant lapse rate, cumulus can get carried away with their own enthusiasm, bunching and building to form first *cumulus-congestus* and then *cumulonimbus*. These are the monsters of the whole cloud family: the thunderclouds. Their upward development is colossal: a strong cumulonimbus (usually shortened to cu-nimb) can reach from ground level to 40,000 ft or more.

These clouds harbour great energy, and there are often strong gust fronts in their vicinity which can change the wind direction and multiply its speed in seconds. Inside it is even worse, with uncontrollable lift and sink, rain, hail and lightning. Cu-nimbs are life-threatening. As a paramotor pilot you will not be tempted to stay in the air dangerously close to a cu-nimb, but you do need to be aware that their activity can set up gust-fronts many miles away. If you are in clear conditions well to one side of anything that looks as if it could be a thunderstorm, be prepared for rapid wind changes in both direction and speed.

Orographic cloud

Any moist air that is cooled to its dew point will form cloud. Air which is forced to move upwards on the windward side of hills or mountains is often cooled enough to form local *orographic* cloud.

Lenticular cloud and wave activity

Lenticular clouds are associated with wave activity in the atmosphere. Lenticulars are smooth-edged and can occur at almost any height with the right combination of local geography and weather conditions. In its simplest form, wave occurs downwind of a hill or mountain ridge. The wave sequence is started when the air meets the ridge and is forced upwards over it.

Lenticular clouds photographed in the evening. There can be ground-level disturbance miles down-wind of formations like this.

CHAPTER 8

Orographic cap cloud formed by moist, warm air being forced up to colder levels on encountering the mountain.

Normally, it will just flow down the other side and the wave will diminish. However, if the atmosphere contains layers of stable and unstable air, the wave may become amplified, particularly if there are further ridges downwind which coincide with the wavelength.

The tops of the waves are often revealed by the presence of lenticular clouds, caused by the condensation of moisture in the upwardly deflected stable layer. They get their name because with a little imagination they can be seen to have a section like that of a magnifying lens. As you would expect, really high waves involve really strong winds, but even at the moderate speeds which paragliders operate in, height gains of several thousand feet are possible from hills only a few hundred feet high.

A very small change in wind speed can make a big difference to the way the wave behaves, because it depends on being in phase with its surroundings. Wave can come and go quite rapidly.

From a paramotoring point of view, wave can be a mixed blessing. Even if you are not interested in it as a potential source of free lift, it is important that you are able to recognise when it may be present because it can also be a source of severe sink and turbulence. This will be on the lee side of the hills developing the wave, and can easily occur many miles away. You may be enjoying some pleasant evening flying in a farmer's field, with a light wind blowing and distant hills no more than a dark line on the horizon. Maybe you have had a couple of nice easy flights and decide to have just one last one before packing up. All goes well until you are making your final approach, when you suddenly have trouble penetrating and the wing seems to have a mind of its own. After a much more untidy landing than you expected, you observe bands of lenticular cloud between you and the hills which had escaped your notice previously. The roughness was almost certainly the effect of the downward element of wave coming into phase with your field.

Rain

The droplets of condensed moisture which form clouds are absolutely minute: so small that they have difficulty in escaping from the cloud mass. Most remain within it, with those at the edges constantly evaporating into the surrounding drier air. However, they can eventually group together to build into much larger drops, and when that happens, rain is the result.

Katabatic flows

A katabatic wind is simply cool air flowing downwards. You are most likely to meet this during evening flights in hilly country. Cool air above the hills will tend to subside down into still-warm valleys. The effect can be particularly noticeable on an eastern-facing slope, which will pass into shadow much sooner than the other side of the valley as the sun goes down. As a paramotor pilot you should be aware of this and be prepared to meet areas of powerful sink close to such faces, even though the general conditions may appear mellow.

Weather forecasts

Once upon a time Britain used to have a reasonably effective free public weather-forecasting service. Met men and women used to appear nightly on television and present synoptic charts with accurate isobars on them, from which it was possible to deduce a reasonable picture of the coming weather. That has now changed to the state where we get a succession of character weather-persons whose job is to present a dumbed-down few seconds of weather-waffle. I am cynical enough to believe that this is so that anyone who really needs a forecast will be forced go elsewhere and pay for it, while a generation grows up believing that our climate is made up of 'spits and spots of rain' and 'rumbles of thunder'. I know that there are still reasonable radio forecasts for farmers and inshore sailors, but generally the free services are poor.

Fortunately, there are other sources. The Airmet and Metfax forecasts use premium phone lines, so the cost is significant, but the information is comprehensive and accurate. For both of these services you need to know which numbers will give the type of information you need for the area you are in. A good starting-off point is a call to the Met Office on 08700 750075 to request their current Met Aviation Weather Services Guide.

The BBC's digital 24-hour television news channel now carries quite good forecasts at half-hourly intervals. This represents quite an economical source of information.

There is a lot of weather data to be found on the Internet. The Met Office has a Web service, MetWEB (http://www.met-office.gov.uk/MWIntro/MWIntro.html). There are also several free Web sites which carry detailed charts, and new ones appear regularly.

Some of the daily newspapers still carry forecasts with moderately detailed charts. At least they show the isobars, fronts and pressure centres (but beware: they usually leave out every other isobar).

Finally, there is your own observation and experience. There is often no more reliable guide to local flying conditions.

Instruments and hardware

To many pilots, adding a motor seems to be an invitation to carry on complicating the basically simple activity of paragliding by buying loads of elaborate instruments too. I hope this chapter will help you to choose items which will really help your flying. They needn't cost a fortune.

When considering any instruments or other gadgets which you may have to adjust in flight, try operating them in the gloves you wear when flying. Also, try to avoid any particularly vulnerable-looking switches and knobs which can easily be wiped off if you should stumble on landing (sooner or later, you will). Lastly, bear in mind that water is the natural enemy of electronics, so check that your instruments are at least showerproof.

All instruments must be carried in a way which guarantees they cannot come adrift in flight. Often a safety-line tied to your harness or flying suit is the best answer. If you choose this solution, make sure the line is not long enough to let it or the instrument swing back into the prop.

Altimeter – essential
This is a 'must have' if your flying is going to be able to comply with the terms of the Exemption. You have to know how high you are so that you keep the required ground clearance. You will also probably be flying

Thommen altimeter with wrist-band: a well-proven aneroid instrument

beneath airways at some time, and knowledge of your height is necessary to avoid straying into them. Regardless of the type of altimeter you get, an essential feature is the ability for it to be zeroed easily (see page 147 for details of altimeter setting).

Since before the beginning of powered flight, pilots have used mechanical altimeters working on the aneroid principle. The heart of these is a vacuum chamber, usually with bellows-like walls. As the pressure of the air surrounding the instrument drops, the bellows expands, moving a pointer via a mechanical linkage. Such instruments are reliable and reasonably accurate, and have the advantage of not requiring batteries. Two models are widely used to this day: the Diplex and the Thommen. The Diplex covers 12,000 ft in a single sweep of the dial, so it is hard to read very accurately, but it is perfectly usable. The Thommen comes in a variety of calibrations, but the most popular model records 3,000 ft in one sweep.

Simple vario-altimeter, with leg strap and safety line. The scale at the top gives the rate of climb (or sink). The digital read-out for the altimeter can be set to indicate height above take-off (QFE) or above ambient mean sea level (QNH).

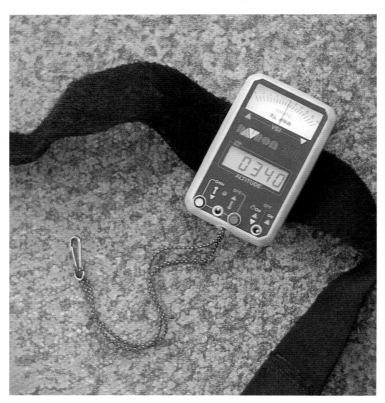

Mechanical altimeters are now becoming obsolete as electronic versions are widely available. These use a pressure-sensitive chip which is usually coupled to a digital display on an LCD screen. They can record altitude differences of as little as a foot. A point to watch out for is that they can be calibrated in feet or metres, and at a glance it is not always obvious which. The better ones allow you to select the units you prefer. However, in paragliding it is unusual to have an electronic altimeter on its own: usually it will be integrated into another pressure-sensitive instrument – the *variometer* (see below).

There are now a number of wrist-watches which incorporate an altimeter function. I have not tried one of these, but all the reports I have seen agree that, at the time of writing, they are generally too slow and imprecise to be relied on when flying.

Variometer

The variometer – normally shortened to 'vario' – measures the *rate* of change of height. They are calibrated in feet per minute or metres per second, and are essential for efficient soaring flight. There is a wide choice on the market, ranging from the simplest, giving just an audible signal (no good at all when your motor is running), to very complex models which can be linked to a GPS system and which store every detail of a flight for printing out later via a computer.

Although you can judge whether or not you are climbing or sinking by looking at the altimeter, it is a lot easier to stay in the best lift if you can read the sensitive display on a vario. If you are completely new to flight, you may be surprised that you need any sort of instrument to tell you whether you are going up or down. In fact, as soon as you are a couple of hundred feet off the ground it is extremely difficult to judge, and at a thousand feet it is quite impossible. It is also nice to be able to use the vario after take-off to monitor and control your rate of climb rather than just keeping the throttle wide open.

New pilots should look for a simple model with a clear display. It will almost certainly incorporate an altimeter, so check that it is easily settable without having to remember endless combinations of buttons. Extra features such as options to record average rates of climb or indicators of speed to glide are not necessary. Go for robustness and clarity. The only extra I really like is the provision of a second battery with the facility to switch to it if the first one fails.

Once you have been flying for a couple of seasons, you may find that the soaring element of your paramotoring is becoming increasingly important. You will be wanting to use the motor to gain height initially and then try to stretch your cross-country performance by exploiting thermal lift. That is the time to think about trading up to a more complex vario – not before.

Compass

In the early days of your flying you will be staying within reach of your take-off site, or at most flying short cross-countries which you can almost memorise from the map. However, as soon as you venture further afield you will find a compass useful. You have a choice between flat or spherical, and in both classes you tend to get what you pay for. The flat compasses produced for orienteering are quite a good compromise as long as you remember that they have to be kept more or less horizontal to work properly.

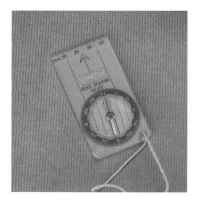

A very basic orienteering compass can work surprisingly well as long as you arrange to mount it horizontally.

Spherical compasses range from the cheap ones from motor accessory shops right up to large and expensive ones made for the boating market. The latter are compensated, well-damped and easy to read. They will work at almost any angle, and until a year or two ago I would have suggested buying a good one if you were going to do any reasonable amount of flying. That was before the cost of GPS instruments came within reach of most of us. These do most of the work of a compass (as long as you are moving) and a lot more besides.

Read on …

GPS

GPS stands for Global Positioning System. The GPS instruments used by paramotor pilots are only about the size of a mobile phone, yet they are capable of indicating your position almost anywhere on earth with an accuracy of 50 metres or less. They can also show altitude, although this function is not quite as reliable as the position one. The system works by obtaining continuous radio fixes from a collection of satellites travelling in orbits 20,000 km above the earth for the benefit of the US military, but now of service to us all. The true beauty of the system is that it is continuous, so you can get accurate readings of the speed you are travelling over the ground. On a slow-flying aircraft such as a paraglider this is a great benefit, particularly when trying to make way into a headwind.

Having declared my enthusiasm for GPS, I have to admit that they are not all plain sailing – not to begin with, anyway. Certainly, to use one simply as a glorified compass is very easy, but getting the best out of them takes a bit of learning. And there lies the problem for the newcomer: even the cheapest GPS instruments contain a vast range of features and it takes practice to find out how to use them fluently.

One of the popular Garmin GPS instruments. The screen shown here displays the 'Highway' display, which is very handy for paramotoring. By simply keeping the road in the centre of the screen, you know that you are flying straight to your destination.

The most popular make among hang-glider and para-glider pilots worldwide is the Garmin. There are several models, and the range is constantly being uprated and refined. It is possible to get one with the complete UK air map already in its database, and at first sight this is an attractive option. However, as the display area is only about 20 cm² it is not easy to read, even though there is a built-in zoom feature.

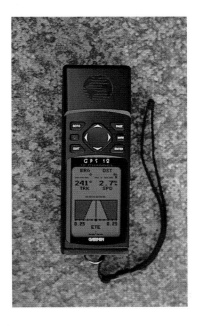

For a typical paraglider flight it is probably more useful to pre-plan your route on an up-to-date air map and mark a few points on the edge of any space you do not want to stray into as waypoints. You can then set up even the simplest Garmin to signal when you are in the proximity of any of those points.

The model I use samples twelve satellites. It needs to be able to 'see' the sky, so it works OK through glass, but not in the middle of my car. I am told that GPS can be reluctant to work below really stormy weather, but you wouldn't want to fly in that anyway. I mention using it in the car because this is a good way of getting used to its features (it can be a practical guide too). GPSs need quite a lot of power compared with, say, the variometer, so it is worth getting one which can use an external power source. That will save a lot of batteries when you are playing with it in the car.

As soon as you become the owner of a GPS you will keep meeting people who insist that there are ways of getting their accuracy down to the width of your toe-nail. There apparently are, but don't worry about it – for paramotoring the accuracy of a standard model off the shelf is more than accurate enough.

Altogether, you should look on the GPS as a really useful accessory to cross-country flight but not as an essential. It does not replace your air map, because it is difficult to read a large enough area. Also, it is rather expensive to keep the map models updated. It does not replace the compass, because that function only works when you are moving; it does not replace the altimeter because the alti feature has been known to be unreliable. Having said all that, I think GPSs are great, and once you get into it you will really enjoy using one.

In paramotor competitions the use of GPS is frequently forbidden because it removes so much of the skill element from navigation.

Airspeed indicator
A few years ago, before the arrival of affordable GPSs, I would have put an airspeed indicator (ASI) quite high on the list of things to own. Nowadays, unless you are testing a paramotor outfit for a magazine or something like that, knowledge of your airspeed when flying is relatively unimportant.

Until you have built up a lot of experience and can judge the breeze confidently, it is useful to know the speed of the wind in your launch place. There are several hand-held instruments which will tell you this. They fall into two categories: mechanical and electronic. Of the mechanical ones, the Swedish Ventimeter is simple and reliable, although rather bulky. It consists of a tapered transparent cylinder with a wire guide up the middle and air inlet and outlet holes at bottom and top respectively. A horizontal disc is free to slide up the wire, and when the instrument is held into wind the height of the disc gives the wind speed, which can be read against a scale on the side of the cylinder. The 'Hall', from the USA, is similar, while the 'Dwyer', also American, uses a tiny plastic ball as the indicator.

The Skywatch ASI in use.

The electronic instruments are very small and handy. They consist of a little ducted fan, which is spun by the wind, and simple circuitry to translate the revs into speed for display on a small LCD screen. The read-out can be in kph, mph or metres/second, so check what you are buying. I use one called a Skywatch, which is still giving excellent service in spite of having survived a session in the washing machine after I accidentally left it in my flying-suit pocket. (This is not a recommendation for anyone else to try the same: I was amazed when I found that it was OK after a week of gentle drying out!)

Engine monitoring instruments

I have seen paramotors fitted with rev-counters and cylinder-head temperature gauges (CHTs). I think this is an area where it is easy to get involved in extra technology just for the sake of it, but some of the instruments are so small and simple that they can be worth having for your peace of mind. I like the neat little Tiny Tach digital rev-counter, which is ideal for paramotor use. It doubles as an engine-hours recorder, which is well worth having, and is a 'fit and forget' piece of equipment. It simply counts the pulses from the ignition lead, and there are models available for single- and twin-cylinder two-strokes.

The matchbox-sized Tiny Tach, which is a combined rev-counter and engine-hours meter.

If you are developing or modifying a power unit, a CHT gauge is necessary, but it shouldn't be required on a sorted-out commercial model.

Flight deck
If you are going to fly cross-country, you will need a map-holder. There are several types available; the main thing to look for is the ease with which it can be clipped onto your harness. To some extent it is a matter of 'the bigger, the better', so that a good area of map is visible. Remember that any pencils you may use with it must be tied on securely.

Radios
A radio is potentially very useful, particularly if you like to fly cross-country. However, in the UK the use of radios from any aircraft is tightly controlled, and you need to know the legal requirements before you purchase. A few AM channels have been allocated for sport aviation: the one for paragliding and hang-gliding is 118.675 MHz, and that appears to be the one most appropriate for PPG use. The radio should be a model approved by the CAA and needs a station licence issued by the Radio Communications Agency. You, the operator, require an RT licence which is obtained after taking a simple test administered by the BHPA. If all these formalities tempt you to take the illegal route of using a 2-metre FM radio, you need to be aware that the penalty for using one may be substantial: a fine of up to £5000 or six months in prison.

Rules, laws and airspace

Flight is an immense freedom, but it is not an unlimited one. As soon as you take off in any type of aircraft, you are bound by the air laws of the country you are flying over. In this sense, paragliders are no different from any other type of flying machine. It is essential that air laws are respected scrupulously if we are to maintain reasonable limits to our flying freedom.

Before going on to the dry details of the rules and regulations, consider the reasons behind some of them:

- Aircraft must avoid collision at all costs.

- Almost anything falling from an aircraft is a threat to life underneath.

- All pilots are hampered by blind spots in their vision; paramotor pilots are better off in this respect than any others, but you need to remember that, just because you can see another aircraft, its pilot cannot necessarily see you.

- There are areas on the ground over which it would be dangerous to fly, such as military firing ranges.

- Some people lack imagination to the extent that they will do really stupid things. Laws don't stop this, but they help a bit.

Where the term *paramotor* is used in this chapter, it refers to all Foot-launched Powered Aircraft (FLPAs) covered by the Exemption.

Basic rules

The Air Navigation Order contains the umbrella of laws which apply to flight in the United Kingdom. As soon as you decide to fly a paramotor you become bound by these laws, although most of them are obviously drawn up with larger, fixed-wing powered aircraft in mind. In the eyes of the law you are a 'commander of an aircraft', and as such you must accept certain legal responsibilities. For example, you must satisfy yourself before take-off that 'all the equipment required for the flight is in a fit condition for use'. Therefore the pre-

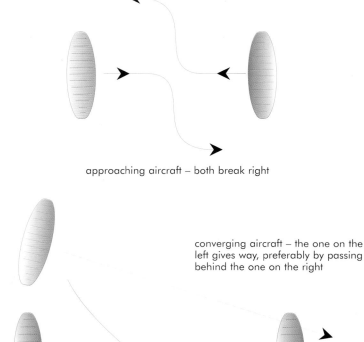

approaching aircraft – both break right

converging aircraft – the one on the left gives way, preferably by passing behind the one on the right

Figure 16: Collision avoidance

flight check is more than a good idea – it is a legal necessity. Once in the air you must not 'recklessly or negligently cause or permit an aircraft to endanger any person or property', so don't even think of buzzing onlookers. You must not be under the influence of drink or drugs. Keep at least eight hours between consuming any alcohol and flight – preferably longer.

A useful source of air-law facts is the book published by the CAA, *CAP 85*. This is primarily for students entering the private pilot maze, but much of its contents are directly applicable to paramotoring. It is a great help if you are taking the BHPA's pilot rating system exams, as is the training issue of the BHPA's magazine *Skywings* and Brian Cosgrove's *Microlight Pilot's Handbook*, currently in its sixth edition. The *UK Air Pilot* is the bible of flight in the British Isles. This is a weighty and expensive book which is updated several times each year. Your nearest central library should keep a copy.

Anti-collision rules
This is a refresher.

These rules are simple, and you *must* know them and use them instinctively:

- Aircraft flying towards each other – **break right**

- Aircraft on converging courses – **the aircraft on the right has priority**; the other one must change course

- On approach and landing – the lower aircraft has priority

- FLPAs give way to **all other aircraft**.

Aeronautical charts
To fly legally, you must not stray into controlled airspace. When you are training and doing circuits there should be no problem. However, as soon as you start to think about cross-country flight, even in the form of

Detail of a 1:250 000 aeronautical chart

quite short hops, you need to know where you can fly. The information is all on the aeronautical charts which are published by the CAA.

Your first sight of one of these 'air maps' can be a daunting experience, leaving you with the impression that the entire country is covered by an invisible labyrinth of such complexity that you will never make sense of it. But it really isn't as bad as it looks. Much of the labyrinth is at heights which you are unlikely to achieve, and once you have gained a little knowledge of the symbols and abbreviations on the chart, you will soon understand it. Also, don't imagine that you have to commit the whole lot to memory. The chart is a reference source which you should use frequently. Until you can contemplate really long cross-country flights, you will do better to transfer its information onto a local map with a larger scale, rather than trying to read it in flight.

The key at the bottom of the map sheets contains loads of useful information, and unless you are map-reading almost daily, you will need to freshen up your knowledge from it quite often. The charts are quite large and it is not unknown for pilots to cut the bottom part off to make them more manageable. This is usually regretted later.

CHAPTER 10

Abbreviations

Aviation jargon is littered with abbreviations. You never stop tripping over new ones, but here are some of those you need to know for a start:

AIAA Area of Intense Aerial Activity

AMSL Above Mean Sea Level

ANO Air Navigation Order

ATZ Aerodrome Traffic Zone

CTA Control Area

CTR Control Zone

FIR Flight Information Region

FL Flight Level

FLPA Foot-launched Powered Aircraft

ICAO International Civil Aviation Organisation

IMC Instrument Meteorological Conditions

MATZ Military Aerodrome Traffic Zone

NOTAM Notice to Airmen

PHG Powered Hang-Glider

PIC Pilot In Command

PPG Powered Paraglider

TMA Terminal Manoeuvring Area

VFR Visual Flight Rules

VMC Visual Meteorological Conditions

Units

On aeronautical charts, in line with international aviation convention, heights are measured in feet, horizontal distances in metres and kilometres or nautical miles, and speeds in knots (nautical miles per hour). Sport pilots in Europe tend to use metres for height and metres per second for speed.

How the air is carved up

It is impossible to cover all the intricacies of air charts in a book such as this, but here is a start:

In Britain, like many other countries, airspace is classi-fied under the ICAO system. This has seven categories. They are marked on the charts by the class letter boxed in blue:

Class A: All the major airways. The flight levels of these are given on the chart and it is usually possible to fly safely underneath them. The rules for general access to Class A airspace are complex and depend on the use of radio for contact with air-traffic controllers.

Class B: Effectively this is all UK airspace above flight level 245 (think of it as 24,500 ft) so don't stay awake at night worrying about what you will meet if you stray into it one day.

Class C: There is no Class C airspace over the UK, but you can find some in Eire where it appears frequently as the lower part of airways and control areas. Avoid.

Class D: A common category covering many control areas and control zones around regional commercial airports. The Exemption is rather ambiguous about these. It suggests that you may enter control zones with the permission of the appropriate air-traffic control unit, but to do that would require passage through control areas, which is forbidden. If in doubt, keep out.

Class E: Belfast TMA and most of the Scottish TMA.

Class F: Advisory airspace. You can think of this as low-grade airways in which all the traffic will be flying according to VFR. This airspace is shown as single lines on the chart, but you should visualise the routes as being normal airway width. Keep out.

Class G: The rest! You may fly freely here provided you take account of all the other users and the mass of restricted space such as that above small airfields, military airfields and Danger Areas – see next section – which share Class G. The rule is 'see and be seen'.

Other areas of restriction

By the time you read through the list from A to G, you could be forgiven for thinking that was everything. Unfortunately there are all sorts of other hazards about which you must be aware:

Aerodrome Traffic Zones (ATZ)

Think of these as transparent vertical cylinders 2000 ft high, centred on the longest runway. If that runway is less than 1850 metres long, the zone will have a radius of 2 nautical miles. If the runway is longer, the radius will be 2.5 nautical miles. I wonder if you find this wild mixture of units as irritating as I do? You cannot glide into or through an ATZ without air-traffic control clearance, and are not even allowed to enter them at all in a PPG.

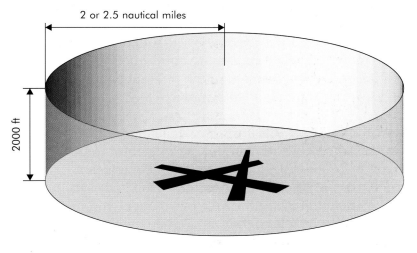

Figure 17: Aerodrome Traffic Zones (ATZ)

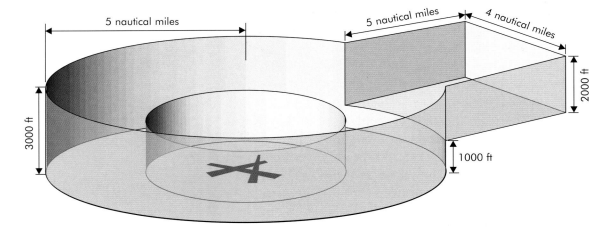

Figure 18: Military Aerodrome Traffic Zones (MATZ)

Military Aerodrome Traffic Zones (MATZ)
Military airfields will have an ATZ of similar size to civil ones, but this is surrounded by a larger zone designated a MATZ. Typically, these are 3000 ft high and 5 nautical miles in radius. In addition there will be an aerial stub 4 nautical miles wide and 5 nautical miles long which extends the MATZ in line with its principal runway (see Figure 18). You may not enter these. The good news is that MATZs are frequently inoperative at weekends and national holidays. Don't gamble on this – your club should have details.

Danger areas (D), Weapons Range Danger Areas (WRDA), Restricted Areas and Prohibited Areas
These are frequently the spaces above military firing and exercise areas, or hazardous industrial places such as nuclear reactors. They are easy to identify on the chart, and their effective altitude above mean sea level is indicated by the figure after the reference number. This gives the altitude in thousands of feet.

Not all Ds and WRDAs are active at all times; those with a star before them are not permanently operative. Full details of timings can be found in the relevant section of the *UK Air Pilot*. Apart from the in-the-air risks connected with overflying these areas, you need to know exactly where they are and be confident of not landing in them because of the danger from unexploded ordnance – this is in addition to the possible legal consequences and the bad reputation you would get for the sport.

Microwaves

This is the casual name for High Intensity Radio Transmission Areas (HIRTAs). On the chart they look like small Danger Areas, but if you take a second look you will see that they are hatched all over, rather than shaded at the edges. The figure after the name indicates the effective height AMSL. If you find your variometer apparently going mental part-way through a cross-country flight, it could be due to the emissions from a HIRTA – they can be powerful enough to scramble instruments. Check the chart!

Non-ATZ airfields etc

The chart will reveal all sorts of bases for aerial activity such as gliding centres, microlight fields, farmers' airstrips, bird sanctuaries and so on. You need to be able to identify all of these and to respect the users.

Remember that you must not fly your paramotor over any built-up areas or gatherings of more than a thousand people.

Ground signals

There are a number of methods of signalling to aircraft. As a paramotor pilot who does not and should not use established airfields you do not need to learn all of them, but there is one you should know about – particularly if you make cross-country flights. Imagine you have strayed from your route a little and see a red flare or repeated red flashes in groups of three: if this is coming from anything resembling an aerodrome, it means **do not land**. You should interpret it as 'clear the area as soon as possible'.

Altimeter settings

To keep within permitted airspace, you must know your height above the ground as well as your position, so an altimeter is essential.

The altimeters we use work by measuring air pressure and translating this information into a height reading. If the air pressure was equal throughout the world, life would be very simple: altimeters could be set to the altitude of the manufacturer's factory and would not need further adjustment. Unfortunately, a change in air pressure of only one millibar will shift an altimeter's reading by about 30 ft (10 m may be easier to remember), so the ability to adjust the setting is essential.

There are three settings you need to know about. To describe them the 'Q' code is used, which takes some getting used to:

- QFE setting is when the altimeter is set to zero on the field you are operating from. Imagine you zero your altimeter, take off and climb until it shows 300; in aviation terms you are flying at a *height* of 300 ft.

- QNH setting is when the pressure adjustment of the altimeter is set to the pressure prevailing at sea level at the time (Area QNH). If the site you are launching from is 300 ft high, on QNH setting your altimeter will show 600 ft after a similar 300 ft climb. You are correctly described as flying at an *altitude* of 600 ft – even though your ground clearance is only 300 ft.

- The third setting is Standard Pressure Setting, or Pressure Altitude. You need to know about it and to understand how it affects many of the airspace markings on the map. Here the altimeter is set to the International Standard Pressure setting of 1013.2 mb. Aircraft using this setting are said to be at the indicated *flight level* (FL). This is the setting used by all powered aircraft once they are at a nominal 3000 ft altitude. On the aeronautical chart, FLs are used to show the upper and lower limits of airways. They are written in multiples of one hundred feet, so *FL* 85 means 8500 ft as shown on an altimeter set to 1013.2 mb. There are rules about the transition between QFE and Pressure Altitude settings, but they are beyond the scope of this book.

Pressure settings

Here's a practical example of why knowledge of the settings is needed: the figures are approximate.

Imagine your flying field is situated 500 ft above sea level and is under an airway. The lower level of the airway is shown on your chart as FL40. Fine, you think, 'I can climb 3500 feet before reaching controlled airspace'. *Not necessarily*. That airway base figure will go up and down according to the Area QNH at the time. Only if that happens to be 1013.2 mb will there be 3500 ft available to you. For each millibar that the QNH is lower, the base of the airway will be 30 ft nearer to the field. Therefore if it is 1003.2 mb, a climb of only 3200 ft will take you into controlled airspace. It works the other way too, so on an very high-pressure day of 1023.2 mb QNH you would have 3800 ft to play with.

Once you appreciate how indicated altitudes are affected by pressure, the reason for the 'flight level' system in which all the aircraft using airways set their altimeters to the same pressure becomes obvious.

Temporary airspace restrictions

Certain restrictions are placed on airspace on a day-to-day basis: royal flights, with their attendant purple airways; air shows, etc. This all comes under the heading of *Temporary Restricted Airspace*, and in Britain you can obtain daily updates free of charge by telephoning 0500 354802.

Military Low Flying – telephone notification

If your paramotoring area is likely to be in airspace shared with fast military jets flying at low level, you can reduce the risk of catastrophe by using the telephone warning system which was originally set up for the use of crop sprayers but was long ago extended to cover other air users. The free phone number is 0800 515544. The system needs at least four hours notice if it is to have any effect, and you really should phone the evening before flying. You will need the grid reference of the site you will be taking off from. Don't imagine that military pilots who are alerted to your activity will leave the airspace free for you alone: they will simply be a bit more likely to be looking out for you. Never be shy about phoning this number: use it!

Don't mix in

Military low-level flying can occur almost anywhere in the UK, between ground level and 2000 ft. Most of the activity takes place between 250 ft and 500 ft, and all civil pilots are advised to avoid this height band whenever possible.

Summing up

Even if your flying is going to be restricted to circuits of a field, you must know if there are any limitations prevailing. If you are considering anything more ambitious, the knowledge to decipher an aeronautical chart and use the resulting information is essential.

And a final thought: an out-of-date chart is almost as useless as none at all. Each chart is revised on a two- or three-year cycle and carries an edition number, so make sure you are using the latest one. If in doubt about this, check with the CAA chart suppliers, Westward Digital Ltd (address on page 186).

Competitions

This is a great time to become involved with paramotor competitions. It is still basically an amateur sport, and any pilot with some skill, some courage and the imagination to exploit the air can become a champion.

An airborne cameraman at the World Air Games in Turkey. The rules for international competitions are very similar to those of the UK championships.

The UK national championship covering paramotors is organised by the BMAA as Class 1 of the Foot-launched Microlight Championships. It takes the form of a series of competitions which are conducted in different parts of the country throughout the spring and summer months. It is open to members of the BHPA too. In addition, there is an annual cross-country league recognised by the BHPA for the Northern Paramotors Cup.

UK national championship

In the UK championship the emphasis is on personal airmanship and navigation by traditional methods, so radios and GPS are forbidden. The rules are based on the ones used in FAI international championships. There is a very interesting menu of tasks from which the competition director can select the ones that are most suited to the area and conditions. There are three categories, and each round of the championships has to include at least one of each:

- limited-fuel tasks

- unlimited-fuel tasks

- precision-flying tasks.

In the total championship, half the tasks have to be unlimited-fuel tasks, with the remainder split between precision and limited-fuel.

The expression 'deck' is used in some of these descriptions. This is an area a hundred metres square which is marked out on the flying field. Normally, all take-offs have to be made from the deck.

All the tasks have a possible maximum of 1000 points. In several of them, some of the score is given for making a clean launch, e.g. 300 for clean take-off at the first attempt, 200 for take-off at the second attempt and 100 for take-off at the third attempt.

Here is an overview of some of the tasks, so that you can get an idea of the type of flying you will have to be good at in order to compete. Some are deceptively simple: for instance, 'Precision take-off and landing'. This is not timed; all you have to do is make a clean take-off, climb to 500 ft, cut the motor and glide via a gate to land as close as possible to a given spot. It is the sort of thing you can perform every time in your home field, but in a strange place with the observers looking on it is all too easy to blow the first launch or try too hard for a dead-centre and stumble on the target. Either way, it'll cost lots of points.

Precision circuit

This is a low-level exercise in which you have to take off and fly so that you can kick a series of nine targets as fast as you can. The targets are each two metres high and approximately 50 metres apart, and have to be struck in the right order. There is also a pylon which has to be flown round in a prescribed direction.

Slow/fast

This is another of the deceptively simple precision tasks. A course 25 m wide and between 250 m and 500 m long is laid out. The task is to fly it first as fast as possible while keeping within 2 m of the ground, and then to make another pass, this time flying as slowly as possible. You are not allowed to zigzag. The object is to get the greatest possible time variation between the two passes. There is a great temptation to fly too close to the stall on the slow pass. Needless to say, no points are gained for touching the ground.

Pure economy

The description is a simple one: just launch with a given amount of fuel and stay up as long as possible before returning to the deck. Again, the simplicity is deceptive: assuming there is any thermal activity, the task is a trade-off between climbing engine-off in thermals, which will be travelling downwind, and powering back to stay within reach of the deck.

Economy and distance

With a given quantity of fuel, fly as many circuits as possible around a short triangular course (under 1 km). Your height is limited to 200 ft, reducing to 30 ft at the pylons. This leaves little scope for thermalling, so it is a fairly pure test of how well the motor and wing are matched for efficiency and how smoothly the pilot can fly.

Economy and navigation

With a given quantity of fuel, fly a given course and identify as many as possible from an unknown number of ground markers and turn points distributed along it. The initial point of the track may be remote from the field, and the pilot has to land back at the deck to score at all.

Economy and precision

In my early hang-gliding days we would have called this 'duration and spot'. You have to make a clean launch, remain aloft as long as possible on a given amount of fuel and then land on a marker on the deck. There are extra points for shutting off the motor at least 5 metres above the marker.

Pure navigation

This is like the economy and navigation task described above, but with a time limit rather than a fuel limit.

Compound navigation tasks

Navigation along a set course can be mixed with pure speed, precision landing and/or deviation from estimated speed to produce different tasks.

Kicking sticks

These are sticks two metres high placed at the corners of a 50 m square. The task is to kick three of the four in a prescribed order as quickly as possible. This is not used as a task in isolation, but as an activity to separate elements of other tasks. The time is integrated into the overall task. It is trickier to achieve than it appears, especially if there is any thermal activity about.

The national cross-country league

Formal competitions are not to everyone's taste, so it is easy to see the appeal of the national cross-country league which is sponsored by Northern Paramotors and run under the auspices of the BHPA. This is a very easy-to-enter competition which you fly whenever you wish during the competition year, which usually runs from the beginning of November one year to the end of October the next. The object is to record the maximum possible distance from a total of six flights. The minimum accepted is 30 km. Once you have registered six flights, you can still improve your score by adding longer ones and discarding the shorter. A great attraction is that the flights don't have to be straight lines: you are allowed to record up to two turnpoints and score the total distance flown along whatever course you wish. This allows out-and-returns, triangles or a couple of dog-legs. All flights must be legal, so naturally fuel is limited to the UK-permitted maximum of 10 litres.

Each flight needs a witness of launch and landing. If turnpoints are involved, they must be photographed from what is known as the 'FAI sector' (see panel on page 156) to prove that they have been rounded correctly. With the increasing adoption of GPS by paramotor pilots, it is probable that GPS records downloaded to a PC may be accepted sometime in the future. Meanwhile, the camera is an essential tool.

Lunging for a target stick at the PPG World Championships in Hungary

The FAI sector

You will meet the expression 'FAI sector' in connection with taking photos for flight verification in all sorts of competitions. It isn't complicated, but a surprising number of competitors get confused about it. The photo sector is an imaginary quadrant (90-degree sector) on the ground with its apex at the turnpoint. It is oriented symmetrically to and remote from the two legs of the course which meet at the turnpoint. Its radius is usually specified at 1 km, although strictly speaking that requirement applies only to international championships. If possible the turnpoint should be one specific corner of a square or rectangular building. In any case it must have a vertical feature.

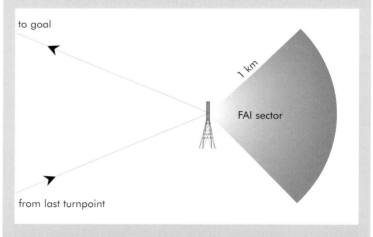

to goal

1 km

FAI sector

from last turnpoint

Figure 19: The FAI photo sector

Bearing in mind that paramotors are not permitted to fly closer than 500 ft to any structure, nor over any congested area of any city, town or settlement, you need to take a bit of care in selecting and photographing your turnpoints.

A brief market review

The world paramotor market is still quite small, and companies come and go frequently. Italy and France have been the homes of much of the development, but there are dozens of manufacturers spread throughout Europe and elsewhere. The choice of which model to buy is very difficult and it can often make more sense to compromise a little and go to a local maker or importer, rather than trying to buy the 'ideal' machine and finding later that spares and service are non-existent in your part of the world. I have confined this list to makers which have sold in reasonable quantities on the British market.

Part of the Adventure range

Adventure (France)

Adventure paramotors are produced in France and imported into the UK by Sky Systems. The F1 is the bottom of the range and uses the popular Solo 210 motor. This is a direct-drive unit, with the prop mounted straight on the end of the crankshaft. Very simple, but inefficient compared with the F2, which has a belt reduction drive, allowing more efficient propeller speeds and quieter operation. Electric start is an option throughout the range, as is a choice of two-blade or four-blade props. All the Adventure units are finished to a very high standard. Adventure can supply wings which have been developed for use with their power units. The Perf gained a good reputation for speed and handling; it has recently been superseded by the Elle.

Air et Aventure (France)

Another French company. Their paramotors are all called Saturne, which is a bit confusing. At the top of the range the Saturne 100K and 110K both use the smooth three-cylinder König motor driving the prop direct from the crankshaft. The 110K has enough thrust for tandem flying. The frames are a typical French design, with high hang-points. This gives good stability, but limits weightshift control greatly. The Saturnes have been around long enough to be safely described as 'well proven'.

The König-powered Saturne from Air et Aventure. The composite plastic prop is of scimitar design with air-dam tips to increase efficiency.

Daichi Kosho (DK) (Japan)

DK is a big Japanese manufacturer of karaoke equipment which diversified into paramotors in the early 1990s. Their units are beautifully made and very fully specified, with electric starting, good silencing and a general air of having been care-

The twin-cylinder DK Beat, from Japan; sadly it is out of production at the time of writing. DK motors are often sold with one of the Hathor range of wings, which have been developed especially for them.

CHAPTER 12

fully designed from the bottom up, rather than assembled out of available parts. For several years DK used a neat little horizontally-opposed twin-cylinder motor, but this has given way to a single-cylinder model, the GT, which has excellent performance but lacks the appealing smoothness of the twins. Rumours within the trade suggest that the twins may yet return to the market.

DKs use three-bladed plastic props of the scimitar design. These have the effect of allowing the pitch to increase slightly at cruise speed, so that the revs can be reduced.

DK's Whisper GT, an efficient single-cylinder model

Fly Castelluccio (Italy)
Fly Castelluccio is a very well-established manufacturer in the Italian town of Castelluccio, which has turned out to be one of the world hot-spots for paramotor construction. The range is very comprehensive, using

Solo and Vittorazzi motors for their single-seaters and JPX for the tandem.

This is the top-of-the-range Power K 115 from Fly Products in Italy. The motor is the 3-cylinder König SC 430. Its static thrust is more than 60 kg, meaning that tandem flight is well within its capability.

Much effort has gone into designing the Fresh Breeze's exhaust system: the curved stainless-steel expansion chamber leads into the final horizontal aluminium silencer.

Fly Products (Italy)

This is another Italian company based in Castelluccio. It was formed by a previous partner in Fly Castelluccio, and makes an impressive selection of models, starting with the ubiquitous Solo 210, but with the intriguing three-cylinder König at the top of the range. This radial triple looks like a 'real' aero engine and is extremely smooth and quiet. It has been used by a number of different makers almost since the start of paramotoring. You may now find Fly Products units being sold under the brand name 'Power' in some places.

Fresh Breeze (Germany)

This is another of the Solo-powered designs. However, it sports a special cylinder head and exhaust system to boost the power, and lots of other neat details, all aimed at keeping the weight down. German regulations demand low noise-emission, and the Fresh Breeze is notably good in this respect. The range has become very popular with European competition PPG pilots.

The company has collaborated with the manufacturers of Swing paragliders to design a fast and stable paramotoring wing called the Silex.

La Mouette (France)

As would be expected from this long-established manufacturer of all things related to minimal flying, the La Mouette paramotors are well engineered and attractively finished. The Solo motor features, as with so many of the other makers, but there are also models driven by the much more powerful Zenoah 250.

Fly Products' single-cylinder Power Plus heavy-duty model. The motor is a Zanzoterra of 312 cc.

PAP (Marbella Parapente) (Spain)

The PAP is a very well-finished range which is sold widely in Europe. Its mainstay is the Solo motor, with a twin-cylinder JPX-powered tandem unit also available. PAP components are found in several other manufacturers' products.

Left *and* **below** *Two views of the businesslike twin-cylinder JPX power unit fitted to the largest model of the PAP range*

Rad Aviation (England)

The English Rad Airheart is one of the most simple power units on the market at present. The motor is the 120-cc Swedish Radne two-stroke which incorporates a small cooling fan. Apart from the fact that it has a belt-drive reduction system, the Rad is about as simple as a paramotor unit can be, and, at a claimed 14 kg, may be the lightest available.

The Rad has rather a utility appearance but it works well. The over-the-shoulder cord starter really can be operated in flight, and simple wire extensions to the choke and primer are provided to ensure an easy re-start after long periods of engine-off soaring. This is a feature which is missing from many of the other manual-start machines on the market. The latest models have a slightly more elaborate safety cage than that shown in the photograph, but the philosophy of raw simplicity persists.

Close-up of the lightweight Rad Aviation Airheart. Its Swedish Radne motor is only 120 cc, but it will fly pilots weighing 80 kg without difficulty. Starting is by pull-cord only.

Revolution (Italy/France)

Originally Italian, the Revolution is now produced in France, where it is marketed as the Backbone, but it still uses Italian Vittorazi motors. These are fairly hi-tech by paramotor standards. The designer has used a fast two-stroke motor which delivers a lot of power for its size. The machine has a number of unusual features such as a clutch and water-cooling. The original models were only 66 cc, but were capable of good performance with pilots weighing up to100 kg or so. In 1997 they grew to 80 cc, in which form they have proved capable of powering even tandem outfits in favourable conditions.

The Revolution, a very compact unit

The Revolution uses gearing to reduce the high crankshaft speeds to the lower rate needed to turn the prop efficiently. The transmission is enclosed in an oil-bath gear-case and incorporates the centrifugal clutch, which originally struck me as an unnecessary complication, but it does

The diminutive Rad Airheart being demonstrated enthusiastically by its test pilot

have certain advantages. Electric starting is easy without having to overcome the inertia of a metre or so of propeller, and if you do have the misfortune to trip on landing, the prop is much less likely to be damaged if it is not revolving. The pumped water-cooling system comes as a bit of a surprise, but it plays an essential part in allowing the motor to operate at the fine tolerances which are needed for extracting so much power from a small package. It also has the benefit of reducing mechanical clatter significantly, a task aided by the generous intake and exhaust silencers.

The cage on the Revolution can be dismantled completely for carriage. The smaller models used a framework made of glass-fibre rods supporting a nylon net, but the others have an aluminium frame. Protective bags are supplied for the components of the cage and the propeller. When the unit is broken down in this way, it really can fit into the boot of a very small car with ease.

Vortex (Spain/England)
The Vortex is a Mike Campbell-Jones production from the same firm that makes the Reflex wing. (Don't confuse the Reflex wing with the French paramotor maker of the same name.) It uses a Solo motor and cage components from the Spanish PAP paramotor. The Solo is extensively re-worked to deliver around 20 bhp.

Stretching performance

There are two ways of looking at a paramotor: either as a small, slow aeroplane which has to be driven everywhere under power, or as a soaring machine with auxiliary power which can exploit the free energy available in the air. Exploiting the soaring capability is loads of fun, but you do have to be prepared to handle your wing in rowdy air to make the most of it. Don't let that put you off: if you are flying the right choice of wing and know what is going on around you, there is nothing to worry about.

By the 'right choice of wing', I mean one which is very stable and easy to handle, and with a high resistance to deflation. There was a tendency among some paramotor pilots to use high-performance wings, sometimes old competition ones, simply because they were capable of relatively high top speeds. That is a really bad idea, because they demand very 'active' piloting . Much better to use a solid intermediate wing which you can relax on, knowing that it will not get you into trouble. A third possibility is to fly the Reflex wing, which is built to be flown with a paramotor and can deliver high speeds in safety (see page 25 for more about the Reflex).

Straight-line distance

If you are simply trying to go as far as possible on a tankful of fuel, the obvious route is directly downwind. Let's imagine you set up in a field with an easy 8-mph breeze and have a small tank which normally allows an hour of give-and-take paramotoring. It is a fine day, with cumulus clouds dotted around the sky. From your

Flying tandem

Another way of extending your paramotoring experience could be by carrying a passenger. The idea of sharing the fun of paramotoring is attractive, but should not be lightly undertaken. You will certainly need a large wing which has been designed for tandem use – many manufacturers produce them – a special harness and a motor unit with plenty of power. The launch and landing techniques are naturally more complex than when flying solo, and pilot and passenger need to develop a certain amount of co-ordination.

The normal prelude to tandem paramotoring is a tandem paragliding course at a BHPA school.

Chris Dawes prepares to take the author aloft.

The take-off run. We are both making the mistake of leaning forwards too much, so that the thrust of the propeller is towards the ground rather than horizontal.

We eventually got off the deck!

Below *This ingenious tandem rig allows the pilot (rear) and passenger to spread apart to give room to run without tangling feet at take-off and landing, but to slide closer together for stability in flight.*

Cruising

Final approach

Landing

training experience you know that this means the air will be bumpy, but you are determined to grit your teeth and fly through the lumps. You plan to cruise at about 800 ft, and expect your airspeed will be 24 mph. You know enough to realise that the wind will be stronger at your cruising height – say 12 mph. Add your cruising speed to that, and after an hour you can expect to have covered 36 miles.

Another approach would be to climb much higher and cruise at, say, 3000 ft to get the benefit of a stronger tailwind at altitude – 22 mph. That could give you 46 miles for your tankful. I know that you would use more fuel while climbing, but you would also have an extra two or three miles of glide down from the cruising height. The flight time would still be about an hour.

Those two examples are both typical power pilots' approaches to the task. If you can think like a soaring pilot, you will see each cumulus as the marker of free thermal lift and prepare by checking possible airspace problems along a route of at least 150 miles. Then it is a matter of climbing out until you meet a thermal: this will be felt as a surge from the wing, with perhaps a powerful feeling that you are being turned one way or the other. Reduce power immediately and lean against the turn, braking on that side to enter the rising air. The wing will probably feel as if it doesn't want to play for a few seconds, but if you persist, your altimeter (or preferably, if you are carrying one, variometer) will soon start to show a climb: then your task is to try and remain in the lift. You can do that by circling, or, if the thermal is a good size, by 'S'-turning in it.

After a few turns you will probably lose the first thermals you find, but with a bit of practice you will discover how to gain a couple of thousand feet without taking the motor off tick-over. Thermals get wider and smoother with height, and you should soon find that you reach a height where the air is definitely cooler and maybe a bit damp. You will be well on the way to cloudbase. That is the time to take stock of your posi-

A map-holder is essential for cross-country flight.

tion and set off downwind to find the next thermal.

You have a huge advantage compared with a non-powered paraglider: if you feel that you are running out of height you can simply open the throttle and climb. You have the ability to search large areas for good lift. You will find that you are covering miles along your course even when circling, because the thermals travel almost as fast as the wind. If it is a good day and the thermals are fairly regular, you may feel confident enough to switch the power off completely for most of the flight. Naturally, a motor which is readily re-started in the air is a great advantage. Unfortunately, many are disappointing in this respect. With the right machine and a fine thermic day, a five-hour flight covering 150 miles on a tankful is not at all far-fetched.

Cloudbase

Don't allow yourself to fly into cloud. On a paramotor it is forbidden: you are required to fly within sight of the surface all the time. Below 3000 ft AMSL, you simply have to remain clear of cloud, with a flight visibility of 3 km. From there up to FL100, there has to be 5 km visibility and you must keep 1000 ft clear of cloud vertically and 1500 ft clear horizontally. It would be very unusual to get higher than FL100 in thermal lift in Britain, but if you do, the visibility requirement extends to 8 km.

As a day warms up the thermals get stronger and the cloudbase gets higher. Certain areas will provide reliable places for generation of thermals which can lead to the generation of rows of clouds aligned downwind. These are called 'cloud streets' and are a great sign of consistent lift. You can often observe how they tend to curve slightly according to the alignment of the isobars on the day.

CHAPTER 13

Out-and-return

A really long flight is a good trophy for your logbook, but getting back home can be an expensive and tedious business, so out-and-return or triangle flights are a better challenge. The basic thermalling technique is the same, but there is plenty of scope for low cunning in deciding your turnpoints and choosing the height at which to fly the into-wind parts of the course. Soon you will be choosing routes which will take you over areas of good thermal generation such as dark, ploughed fields. You will learn to exploit the sunny sides of valleys, get a free ride in ridge lift, and all the other skills and techniques of soaring pilots.

The landing field

Cross-country flying inevitably involves landing in fields you have not previously inspected and which you can see only from the air. If you still have fuel and power, your choice is quite wide, but even so you have to be careful how you go about it.

First, absence of livestock – particularly horses – is a must. And don't imagine that you can fly in low and inspect likely places before powering up and climbing out to the next choice: if there is anyone about you can be held to be breaking the conditions of the Exemption which require you to keep 500 ft clearance from people and dwellings except when you are actually landing. There has already been one successful prosecution for doing exactly that.

Flying low over fields isn't a good idea anyway, because of the danger from electric wires. All pilots should have a healthy fear of these. Most of us imagine some sort of horror scenario concerning the multi-megawatt lines carried on giant pylons, but those aren't the ones that cause the accidents because they are so obvious and go in fairly straight lines. No, the wires to watch out for are the sneaky little ones carrying a handful of volts to an isolated farmhouse or milking parlour. These tend to be only twenty or thirty feet up and made of copper which oxidises to a subtle

Navigation

It is very easy to become disoriented when concentrating on the constant turning involved with working thermal lift. With experience, you learn to keep a general sense of where you are by referring to features which may be many miles away, such as power stations or big silos, but the first few times you venture beyond your local fields it is easy to lose touch with familiar features and momentarily panic. In recent years the GPS system has made life much easier, but it is still essential to be able to keep track of your progress on a map.

green: just right to blend in with grass when viewed from above. They can follow lanes or field edges and then dart off on a diagonal without warning. All cross-country pilots develop a technique of surveying possible landing fields for wires by looking for poles and buildings and being very suspicious of what may be between them.

OK, no livestock, no wires; that's it, then? Not quite. You need to approach into wind and preferably not downhill. There are usually clues about wind direction: smoke, flags, cloud shadows, leaves on trees and so on. Also, you should have set up your final approach from a couple of hundred feet, which will allow you to sense the drift and adjust as necessary while you glide in. The slope can be harder to judge, but often there are plenty of clues in the local topography – expect rivers to be lower than roads, and so on. In any case, the glide ratio of a paraglider with the pilot upright in full-drag position and the motor stopped will only be about 4:1, so you can tolerate a bit of down-slope if necessary.

Finally, when you are down safely, pack up and make a point of contacting the landowner and explaining how you came to be in his field. Do this before you pull out your mobile phone and direct your mates to bring their 4WD up the track and through the fields. Oh, and shut the gate! A little thoughtfulness and courtesy pays off. In more than twenty years of hang-gliding and paragliding I have never met a farmer who was upset by my arrival and have received unexpected hospitality more then once.

The Foot-launched Powered Aircraft Training Syllabus

This is the BHPA's full FLPA training syllabus, which may be subject to detail updates. It contains a few items not relevant to PPGs, which you can ignore. If you have read the previous chapters, you should have been introduced to most of the areas of required knowledge. The important thing to remember is that nobody is trying to catch you out for the sake of it. This is simply the knowledge you need to operate a paramotor with regard to your own safety and that of others.

Introduction

This syllabus is set out in two main sections: Ground-school and Practical. Also included [not reproduced here] is a copy of the checklist which instructor(s) should furnish each student with to record their progress through the syllabus. This should be used in conjunction with the usual more detailed individual student records. (These records are especially important where students may visit a hill or tow school for their unpowered training, and then a power school for the power elements.)

General:
A pilot under training will fly under direct instruction from the instructor at all times.

A pilot under training will fly only either within sight of or in pre-arranged radio contact with a designated instructor unless he is performing a declared cross-country task.

No student may fly under power until the required unpowered flight skill levels relating to the required tasks have been fully demonstrated to the satisfaction of the instructor.

All paragliding and hang-gliding skills shall be taught in accordance with the guidance and regulations produced by the BHPA.

A. Groundschool
1. Equipment
1.1 The canopy
1.1.1 Daily checks and pre-flight checks
The student will demonstrate daily and pre-flight checks and demonstrate his knowledge of the materials and methods used in the construction of the canopy.

1.1.2 Maintenance
The student will demonstrate his knowledge of the need for regular inspections and maintenance of his canopy, the harness and the emergency parachute including emergency parachute re-packing.

1.2 Clothing
The student will demonstrate a knowledge of the need for appropriate clothing including helmet, gloves, flying suit etc. No scarves – jacket drawstrings – long hair!

1.3 Instruments
The student will demonstrate the use of an altimeter and a compass and will be able to demonstrate his knowledge of the circumstances in which these should be used.

1 .4   The power unit
1.4.1   Configuration
The pilot under training will demonstrate an understanding of all the component parts of the motor unit and their inter-relationships. Particular emphasis will relate to:

a)   care and balance of propellers

b)   safety cages and the importance of maintaining them in good condition

c)   fuel taps; ignition switches; emergency engine stopping

d)   spark plug and lead

e)   the risk of damage to the motor unit and in particular the throttle cable during transit

f)   correctly rigging the motor to the glider with safety straps in accordance with the manufacturer's recommendations

g)   vibrations, their effects and methods of preventing its consequences.

1.4.2   Mixing fuel
The pilot under training will demonstrate an understanding of:

a)   mixing fuel

b)   different mixtures for running in and subsequent periods and the need to keep an engine time log book

c)   the difference between synthetic and other oils

d)   reasons why petrochemicals and paragliders and hang-gliders don't mix.

1.4.3   Safety

The pilot under training will gain an understanding of:

a)   the need to operate safely and what can go wrong

b)   ways of protecting himself and others during running-in periods – an appreciation of the power generated by the propeller at full engine speed is essential

c)   safety procedures associated with helpers starting the motor unit

d)   procedures in the event of fire

e)   general fitness, eyesight, the effect of drugs, alcohol etc.

1.4.4   Starting procedures

The pilot under training will gain an understanding of starting procedures, including:

a)   clearing the area and clear prop

b)   checking the motor unit to ensure that everything is in its proper place, e.g. plug lead

c)   check the fuel tank contents

d)   fuel tap

e)   choke (where fitted)

f)   pull handle etc.

g)   demonstrate an understanding of the warm-up of the motor for correct running.

2.   Weather
2.1   General weather

The pilot under training will demonstrate a general

understanding of weather patterns, and associated wind direction and strength.

2.2   Weather patterns and forecasts
The pilot under training will demonstrate an understanding of how weather systems affect flying conditions. An understanding of the following will be demonstrated.

2.2.1   Forecasts

2.2.2   Cloud recognition

2.2.3   High- and low-pressure systems and fronts

2.2.4   Unstable weather, turbulence and gust fronts

2.2.5   Stable weather, effect on visibility and inversions

2.2.6   Stable/unstable conditions.

2.3   Local weather
The student will demonstrate an understanding of how the following affect flying conditions.

2.3.1   Airflow on and around hills; katabatic flow

2.3.2   Wind gradient

2.3.3   Turbulence, venturi effect and gusts

2.3.4   Sea breezes

2.3.5   Thermal cumulus cloud development

2.3.6   Standing waves and their effect.

2.4   Weather in XC situations
The student will demonstrate an awareness that powered paragliders and power gliders can fly in locations and maintain height where gliders are not able to do so. The need to maintain an awareness of overall

wind direction and its effect in valley situations will be discussed and wind gradient in different topographical situations considered.

The student will demonstrate the ability to assess suitable flying weather.

3. *Theory*
3.1 Theory of flight – general
The student will demonstrate a knowledge of:

3.1.1 Principles of flight including drag, airflow over the wing, angle of attack, wing loading, glide angle and sink speed

3.1.2 Effect of brakes on angle of attack and speed (powered paragliders). The effects of flying too slowly (the stall)

3.1.3 Air speed – wind speed – ground speed

3.1.4 Emergency and safety procedures.

3.2 Theory of flight – powered paraglider/ powered hang-glider
The student will demonstrate a knowledge of:

3.2.1 Lift, thrust weight and drag and the effect of power on angles of attack

3.2.2 Forces in turns and the effect on stall speed

3.2.3 Climbing and diving turns

3.2.4 Reduction drives

3.2.5 Propeller theory

3.2.6 Torque effects and how these can be controlled

3.2.7   Understanding the trim of the motor and adjusting the thrust line for a particular weight of pilot
and glider (powered hang-gliders). Hang points
– the effect of altering

3.2.8   The effect of speed systems on a powered paraglider under power on and off situations
(powered paragliders)

3.2.9   The effects of weight on flying speed, stall
speed/flare and the need for weight checks
(powered paragliders)

3.2.10 Understand the concept that power equals
climb and bar position equals air speed (power
gliders)

3.2.11 The effect of flying too slowly

3.2.12 Emergency and safety procedures.

3.3   Airmanship

The pilot under training will demonstrate a knowledge
of:

3.3.1   Dangers – powerlines, trees, water

3.3.2   Turbulence and its consequences

3.3.3   Flying with others, anticipation

3.3.4   The emergency parachute

3.3.5   The choice of safe field, including climb-out
clearance ground conditions, turbulence
generators, obstructions and overshoot areas,
including landing-out behaviour

3.3.6   Assessment of conditions for flight

3.3.7   Safe areas for onlookers

3.3.8 Noise nuisance and congested areas

3.3.9 Emergency stopping and take-off abort

3.3.10 Techniques for avoiding – and recovering from where appropriate – tucks, stalls and spins and sudden power loss

3.3.11 Methods of navigation. Planning a 30 km (total) flight either as an out-and-return flight with a predeclared turnpoint or as a flight to a pre-declared goal

3.3.12 Emergency and safety procedures.

3.4   Air law
The pilot under training will demonstrate a thorough knowledge of air law and regulations applicable to powered foot-launched aircraft with specific reference to 'the Exemption' to the ANO including:

3.4.1 Collision avoidance rules

3.4.2 Landing rules

3.4.3 Night (definition of)

3.4.4 Congested areas

3.4.5 500 ft rule (low flying)

3.4.6 Visual flight rules

3.4.7 Purple airways

3.4.8 Notams

3.4.9 Incident reports

3.4.10 Air charts

3.4.11 Thermalling rules

3.4.12 Airspace

3.4.13 Restrictions and hazards

3.4.14 Aerodrome rules, signals and symbols.

B. Practical
4. *Practical*
4.1 Pre-motorised flights
Prior to flying with a motor unit the pilot under training will carry out the following tasks on a paraglider or hang-glider as appropriate:

NB These flights must be supervised by a BHPA Instructor (hill or tow) licence holder in the appropriate discipline.

4.1.1 Demonstrate an effective PLF (not wearing back-pack) (paraglider)

4.1.2 Correctly carry out pre- and post-flight routines

4.1.3 Demonstrate the ability to plan a flight and execute the plan

4.1.4 Demonstrate safe airspeed control

4.1.5 Complete four appropriate controlled landings in a designated area

4.1.6 Consistently demonstrate clean take-offs, good flares and accurate landing into wind

4.1.7 Demonstrate an 'S'-turn flight plan so that a safe landing can be made as if the tow line had failed to release (tow)

4.1.8 Demonstrate safe and effective turn control of the aircraft.

4.1.9   (tow) Complete a minimum of 3 flights and attain self release from a safe height for a stand-ard school circuit on each occasion.
(hill) Complete a minimum of 5 flights with at least 200 ft ground clearance

4.1.10   Demonstrate emergency collapses (paraglider on the ground). Demonstrate a full stall recovery with minimal height loss (hang-glider)

4.1.11   Demonstrate competence at forward and reverse launching and canopy control

4.1.12   Experience take-offs in winds less than and greater than 5 mph

4.1.13   Demonstrate 'big ears' (paraglider)

4.1.14   Demonstrate safety and emergency procedures.

4.2   Motor unit – ground work
4.2.1   Demonstrate pre-take-off control of aircraft

4.2.2   Demonstrate simulated post-landing control of aircraft

4.2.3   Demonstrate competence at parking aircraft safely

4.2.4   Demonstrate knowledge of the following:

– Clearing the fuel supply of bubbles

– Clear prop

– Kill switch and emergency engine stopping

4.2.5   Correctly carry out pre- and post-flight routines

4.2.6   Demonstrate launch abort

4.2.7   Demonstrate safety and emergency procedures.

4.3   Powered flight

NB These flights must be directly supervised by a BHPA Instructor (power) licence holder.

They must not be undertaken until sections 4.1 and 4.2 have been completed.

4.3.1   Demonstrate consistently good launch technique (forward and reverse – paramotor)

4.3.2.   Three consecutive powered flights from a flat site with at least 100 ft ground clearance, with unassisted take-off runs, smooth 90-degree left and right turns including good airspeed and throttle control, and finish with stand-up power-off landings including full deflation of the canopy between flights (powered paraglider)

4.3.3   Complete 3 landings within 20 m of a defined spot in winds of less than 5 mph. Complete 3 landings within 20 m of a defined spot in winds of more than 10 mph

4.3.4   Minimum of 10 flights logged (including full deflation and inflation of canopy between flights) (powered paraglider)

4.3.5   Demonstrate the safe and effective use of 'big ears'

4.3.6   Carry out an accurate power-off landing to the satisfaction of the instructor from at least 500 ft

4.3.7   Demonstrate an ability to fly co-ordinated 360-degree turns in both directions

4.3.8   Complete a 30 km (total) flight with a pre-declared turnpoint or as a flight to a declared goal or a triangle

4.3.9 Display the ability to fly safety with others, maintaining a good look out, complying with the rules of the air and exhibiting good airmanship, and demonstrate an ability to manoeuvre powered paragliders safely, considerately and in accordance with air traffic rules

4.3.10 Must have successfully flown paramotors or paragliders or hang-gliders or power gliders or microlights as pilot in command on at least 8 separate days within the previous 9 months

4.3.11 Must have a minimum of 5 hours logged airtime as pilot in command on paragliders, powered paragliders, power gliders or hang-gliders or microlights of which at least 3 hours must be on powered paragliders or powergliders

4.3.12 Satisfy the instructor that the pilot has the correct attitude to continue a flying career both safely and competently

4.3.13 Pass the BHPA 'Power' written exam.

Glossary

Cross-references are indicated by SMALL CAPITALS.

ACPULS System of flight testing and certification. Originally French.

Aerofoil *see* AIRFOIL.

AFNOR System of flight testing and certification which has superseded ACPULS.

Airfoil Surface which is shaped to provide lift from moving air; in paragliding, the shape of the cross-sections of the wing chord.

Alpine launch The take-off method in which the pilot faces forwards at the start; also called the **snatch** or **forward launch**.

Angle of attack The angle at which the MEAN CHORD of the airfoil meets the airflow.

Aspect ratio The relationship between the span of the wing and its chord. A wing with a big span and a narrow chord is described as having a high aspect ratio.

Backup [system] Reserve parachute.

Big ears Deliberately collapsing the tip cells of the wing to increase the rate of descent.

Blob Small weak thermal or isolated patch of lift.

Brakes Popular but slightly inaccurate term for the aerodynamic controls on a paraglider.

Camber The curve in the airfoil section. On a paraglider it can be altered by applying the BRAKES.

Canopy The entire fabric wing of the paraglider: the expression *wing* is normally preferred in this book.

Cascade failure A series of LINE breaks resulting from progressive overload following an initial break.

Centre of pressure The point in the wing at which the entire aerodynamic force is considered to act.

Chord The measured distance between the leading and trailing edges of a wing.

CIMA The FAI Commission which deals with microlight aircraft – including PPGs.

CIVL Commission Internationale de Vol Libre. The international hang-gliding committee of the FAI, the governing body of both hang-gliding and paragliding.

Core The area of strongest lift within a thermal. There may be several cores in a big thermal. Has produced the verb 'to core': to centre in the lift and climb efficiently.

Coriolis Force The apparent force which deflects wind patterns to the right (clockwise) in the northern hemisphere and to the left (anticlockwise) in the southern one. It is due to the rotation of the earth.

Crab *see* KARABINER.

DHV The German hang-gliding association – providers of a flight-testing system which is an alternative to AFNOR.

Flare To increase the angle of attack rapidly by using both brakes together, usually as the final stage of landing.

Gleitschirm German for paraglider.

GPS Global Positioning System.

Gütesiegel German flight testing and certification seal of approval. Issued by DHV.

IPPI card International Pilot Proficiency Identification card. Issued by national paragliding governing bodies so that clubs and site operators in other countries can be assured of a pilot's standard.

Karabiner Connector with a quick-release gate, normally used to join the harness to the risers.

Land out To make an unscheduled landing anywhere other than at your home field.

Lift band The rising air in front of a ridge which provides sufficient lift for soaring.

Lines All or any of the cords connecting wing and pilot.

Maillon Link ring closed by a screwed nut. Used to connect the lines to a RISER, and sometimes also used instead of KARABINERs to connect the harness.

Mean chord A line passing through the wing section via the centre of the leading edge and the trailing edge. This is the line against which the ANGLE OF ATTACK is measured.

NOTAM Notice to airmen. Official advisory notices issued by the relevant national aviation authority, and covering such things as flying displays, major competitions, NATO exercises etc. NOTAMS come in both permanent and temporary varieties.

Parachutal stall A condition in which the whole wing is stalled, but in which it retains its shape and allows the paraglider to become a parachute, with its high drag causing a vertical descent.

Parapente French for paraglider.

Parascending The original name for paragliding in Britain, when the sport consisted of being towed into the air behind a vehicle and parachuting to the ground. Still used for tow-launched flight of a non-soaring nature.

PLF Parachute Landing Fall. A method of minimising personal injury by preparing to collapse sideways with knees bent and ankles tight together in the event of a heavy landing.

Polar [curve] A graph plotting the sink rate of a glider throughout its speed range.

Porosity The property of a material that allows air to pass through it. For paraglider cloth, the lower the porosity, the better.

Pumping Pulling BRAKES to re-inflate a partially collapsed wing.

PWC Paragliding World Cup annual competition series.

Rescue [system] The expression commonly used in Europe for the BACKUP or reserve parachute.

Reserve Backup emergency parachute.

Risers The lengths of webbing between the harness and the LINES. They will be designated A-risers, B-risers etc from front to rear, according to the set of lines to which they are attached.

Rotor Air turbulence caused by a large obstacle – usually a ridge or range of mountains.

Shooting The tendency for a canopy to surge forwards when recovering from a stall or encountering turbulence.

SIV *Simulation d'incidente en vol*. Usually a course in which canopy collapses, spins and other potential disasters are practised safely, over water.

Stall Sudden loss of lift due to breakup of orderly airflow over the wing.

Tip vortex A spiral of disturbed air flowing behind each wingtip.

Toggle The word used by parachutists for the handles on the control lines (brakes). Hence **toggling** is sometimes used to describe steering.

Tow training A method of teaching paramotoring by tow-launching the trainee into the air on a paraglider. After several flights the motor unit is added but towing continues. Further launches are made, first with a dead engine, then with it running but no propeller fitted. This way the new pilot becomes familiar with launch procedures and throttle and brake control before moving on to normal powered take-offs.

Trim speed The speed at which the paraglider flies 'hands-off'.

Tuck Wing collapse caused by the leading edge collapsing downwards and closing the front of the cells.

Wake turbulence Rough air behind the wing, caused by prop-wash and tip vortices.

Wing *see* CANOPY.

Wraps Temporarily shortening the brake lines by looping them around your hands. Potentially risky in flight but useful when ground handling or just before making a nil-wind landing.

XC Cross-country flight.

Further reading

Books

Tom Bradbury, *Meteorology and Flight*, A & C Black, 1996

Brian Cosgrove, *Pilot's Weather*, Airlife Publishing, 1998

Brian Cosgrove, *The Microlight Pilot's Handbook,* Airlife Publishing, 1998

Ian Currer and Rob Cruickshank, *Touching Cloudbase*, Airlife Publishing, 1996

Dick File and Ian McCaskill, *Weather Facts*, Oxford Paperbacks, 1991

Derek Piggott, *Understanding Flying Weather*, A & C Black, 1996

David Sollom and Matthew Cook, *Paragliding from beginner to cross-country*, Crowood Press, 1998

Noel Whittall, *Paragliding: The Complete Guide*, Airlife Publishing (UK) and Lyons Press (USA), 1997

Magazines

At the time of writing there is no publication dealing exclusively with paramotoring, but it is frequently covered in the following magazines:

Cross-Country (France, but printed in English)

Delta & Parapendio (Italy)

Fly and Glide (Germany)

Para World (Japan)

Paragliding — The Magazine (USA)

Swiss Glider (Switzerland, printed in French and German)

Skywings (UK)

Vol Libre (France)

Yearbook/buyer's guide

World Directory of Leisure Aviation, English-language edition: Pagefast Ltd (also published in French and German)

Useful addresses

British Hang Gliding and
   Paragliding Association Ltd
The Old Schoolroom
Loughborough Road
Leicester
LE4 5PJ
Tel: 0116 261 1322
Fax: 0116 261 1323
e-mail: office@bhpa.co.uk

The British Microlight Aircraft
   Association
Bullring
Deddington
Banbury
Oxon.
OX15 0TT
Tel: 0186 933 8888
Fax: 0186 933 7116
e-mail:
   100772.1123@compuserve.com

British Paramotoring Club*
7 Jubilee Road
Basingstoke
Hampshire
RG21 3DL
Tel: 0125 681 7587
Fax: 0125 647 5076
e-mail:
   info@paramotoring.co.uk

* The BPC is a commercial club.

CAA charts distributed by:
Westward Digital Ltd
37 Windsor Street
Cheltenham
Gloucestershire
GL52 2DG
Tel: 01242 235151
Fax: 01242 584139

Hang Gliding Federation of
   Australia
P O Box 558
Tumut
NSW 2720
Australia
Tel: +61 2 69 472 888
Fax: +61 2 69 474 328
e-mail: hgfa@tpgi.com.au

Hang Gliding and Paragliding
   Association of Canada
#13 13670 84 Ave.
Surrey
British Columbia
Canada
V3W 0T6
Tel: +1 604 507 2565
Fax: +1 604 507 2565

Fédération Aéronautique
   Internationale
Avenue Mon Repos 24
1005 Lausanne
Switzerland
Tel: +41 21 345 1070
Fax: +41 21 345 1077
e-mail: office@fai.org

New Zealand Hang-Gliding and
   Paragliding Association Inc.
P O Box 3521
Richmond
Nelson
New Zealand
Tel: +64 3 540 2183
Fax: +64 3 540 2183
e-mail:
   nzhgpa.admins@clear.net.nz

South African Hang Gliding and
   Paragliding Association
P O Box 1993
Halfway House
1685
South Africa
Tel: +27 11 805 5429
Fax: +27 11 805 5429
e-mail: sahpa@paragliding.co.za

United States Hang Gliding
   Association
P O Box 8300
Colorado Springs
CO 80933
USA
Tel: +1 719 632 8300
Fax: +1 719 632 6417
e-mail: ushga@ushga.org

United States Ultralight
   Association Inc
P O Box 667
Frederick
MD 21705
USA
Tel: +1 301 695 9100
Fax: +1 301 695 0763
e-mail: usuahq@aol.com

Index